Why Are We Yelling?

BUSTER BENSON

*Why Are
We Yelling?*

THE ART OF PRODUCTIVE
DISAGREEMENT

PORTFOLIO / PENGUIN

PORTFOLIO/PENGUIN
An Imprint of Penguin Random House LLC
penguinrandomhouse.com

Most Portfolio books are available at a discount when purchased in quantity for sales
promotions or corporate use. Special editions, which include personalized covers, excerpts,
and corporate imprints, can be created when purchased in large quantities. For more
information, please call (212) 572-2232 or email specialmarkets@penguinrandomhouse.
com. Your local bookstore can also assist with discounted bulk purchases using the
Penguin Random House corporate Business-to-Business program. For assistance in
locating a participating retailer, email B2B@penguinrandomhouse.com.

LIBRARY OF CONGRESS CATALOGING-IN-PUBLICATION DATA
Names: Benson, Buster, author.
Title: Why are we yelling? : the art of productive disagreement / Buster Benson.
Description: [New York] : Portfolio/Penguin, [2019] |
Includes bibliographical references and index. |
Identifiers: LCCN 2019030457 (print) | LCCN 2019030458 (ebook) |
ISBN 9780525540106 (hardcover) | ISBN 9780525540113 (ebook)
Subjects: LCSH: Interpersonal conflict. | Interpersonal communication.
Classification: LCC BF637.I48 B46 2019 (print) |
LCC BF637.I48 (ebook) | DDC 158.2—dc23
LC record available at https://lccn.loc.gov/2019030457
LC ebook record available at https://lccn.loc.gov/2019030458

Printed in the United States of America
1   3   5   7   9   10   8   6   4   2

Book design by Pauline Neuwirth

To Kellianne, Niko, and Louie,

with whom I have my most enjoyable disagreements.

Contents

Why Are
We Yelling?

Introduction

THREE
MISCONCEPTIONS

A weed is but an unloved flower.
—ELLA WHEELER WILCOX

A man is yelling obscenities in his backyard. His neighbor, overhearing this ruckus, walks up to the short fence between their yards and asks if everything is okay.

"No! Everything is *not* okay!" he yells back, before catching his misdirected anger and becoming apologetic. He stands up and tries to shake off his rage. His fists clench giant tangles of pulled weeds: dandelions, sour grass, and other local varieties that the neighbor recognizes as the scourge of homeowners. The man gestures to his garden. "These stupid weeds! How do you keep these pests out?"

The neighbor can tell that he's given his yard a lot of attention, despite his frustration with it. A beautiful lemon tree grows along the back wall, and a variety of flowering plants offer secondary focal points that pleasantly zigzag across the yard, ultimately returning her eye to the lemon tree. She says, "I think you might be pulling them up the wrong way. These plants have long, fragile roots, and their bulbs break off and stay underground. They're sneaky weed hydras: every time you chop off one head, twelve grow back."

THE WEED HYDRA

"Ugh—weed hydras are the last thing I want to deal with right now!" the man says. "I don't have time to excavate each precious weed one by one. I work all day and just want to come home to a nice yard."

AFTER-WORK DESIRES

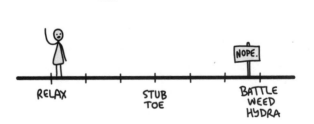

"I can show you how to do it," the neighbor offers. "It can be pleasant work. Also, these weeds you have aren't all bad; they do good things too. Their long roots bring nutrients up to the topsoil and help hold the soil together during rains. And their leaves make a good salad topping."

The man scoffs. "Salad's not my thing. Thanks for the offer to help, but no thanks. I'm just going to do what I always do and then move on to more important things." He yanks a few more weeds out and hurls them into the compost pile with an angry force reminiscent of a knight swinging his sword at a dragon. "Maybe I'll just burn the whole yard to the ground," he mumbles under his breath, and he marches back inside.

Arguments and weeds are similar in many ways. They sprout in our gardens and minds. We usually don't want them in either place; they're nuisances at best and mortal enemies at worst. Many of us approach disagreements the same way this man approaches weeds— as things to battle and destroy.

This book is about the art of productive disagreement, which requires a shift in mind-set akin to the one the man's neighbor tried to suggest. To begin to see it, first we need to remove a few common misconceptions about what arguments really are.

MISCONCEPTION 1

Arguments Are Bad

They're not bad, but they can be unproductive. We aren't taught how to argue productively.

I'M ACTUALLY QUITE FRIENDLY

We argue with our alarm clock, which insists we wake up. We argue with our clothes that wear out or stop fitting. We argue with our bodies, we argue with our pets, we argue with bumps in the sidewalk that we almost trip on, we argue with cars in traffic, we argue with our bosses and teachers and parents, we argue with computers and technology, we argue with our friends and relatives, we argue with our spouses and children, we argue with the television, we argue with the sky. We argue with ourselves. And when we sleep, arguments creep into our dreams as well. No wonder we're yelling—*it's exhausting!*

To add insult to injury, when I asked people what they think about the way we argue, nine out of ten people classified arguments as unproductive.

Why do we argue if it's both unpleasant and unproductive?

THE WAY WE ARGUE IS...

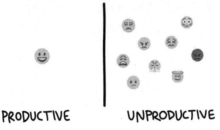

PRODUCTIVE   UNPRODUCTIVE

Despite how pointless they often seem afterward, don't arguments feel unavoidable in the moment? It's true: in the moment, arguments perform a crucial—and underappreciated—job for us by waving a flag that something important to us is being endangered, whether it's a personal preference, a hunch about the best strategy for meeting a shared goal, or a core value of ours. This endangerment sparks strong emotions. Often we notice the emotional buildup and push it back down, waiting for a better time or telling ourselves that it's not worth our energy. And we advise others to pick their battles wisely, doing everything they can to keep the peace. But if we make a habit of pushing the frustration too far down, sometimes we begin to believe *we're* at fault for being frustrated, and we beat ourselves up about it. If we do that, the arguments decrease in frequency, but we're left with a constant low-level anxiety that slowly wears away at our mental and physical health. Today, one in five adults in the United States has some form of anxiety disorder, and the rate of deaths from the three despair-related causes (suicide, drug overdose, and alcohol-related illness) has been increasing for the last decade, causing our average life span to actually dip for the first time in decades. Hiding from our negative emotions doesn't make them go away. They'll find some way out, even if it kills us.

We need weeds, and we need disagreements too. Famous marriage researcher Dr. John Gottman says that a relationship without conflict is a relationship without communication and is bound to fail. Conflict is inevitable whenever two or more people are talking about things from their own unique perspectives. Disagreements are a sign that the relationship's soil is healthy. (Gottman recommends a 5:1 ratio of positive encounters to negative encounters, because this ensures that the flow of disagreements is kept open—and can therefore be resolved without being overwhelmingly negative.)

NOT ENOUGH   JUST RIGHT   TOO MANY

And yet most of us were never taught how to argue. We weren't taught how to navigate negative encounters so that we are able to acknowledge the negative and strengthen the positive. How we argue matters. Luckily, this is a solvable problem. We can learn this skill.

But first: how did I end up obsessed with productive disagreement, and why should you listen to me? When my mom asks me, every couple of years, what I actually do for a living, it's always tough to explain. I've spent the last twenty years as an entrepreneur, engineer, and product leader at high-profile, hyper-growth tech start-ups like Amazon, Twitter, and Slack. I've worked with engineers, designers, marketers, researchers, data analysts, customer support reps, business leaders, and customers—each with different plates spinning, different anxieties clashing, different incentives to pursue, and different measurements for success. My job has basically been to help facilitate meaningful and productive collaboration within a million ever-changing constraints. At the same time, I've been studying cognitive biases, logical fallacies, and systems thinking and applying what I've learned to the work I do. In 2016, I published an article titled "Cognitive bias cheat sheet," which proposed an analysis and simplification of more than two hundred cognitive biases. It went viral and has since been adopted by academics and researchers around the world as a way to reframe cognitive biases. Instead of dismissing them as mental bugs, we should consider that our brains had a very good reason for adopting these shortcuts of thinking. They continue to help us get things done in a world of information overload and scarcity of time and attention. Rather than fighting these short-cuts, our effort will be better spent developing honest bias, which means accepting our own limitations and always remaining open to evidence of our blind spots.

This mix of professional and amateur obsessions has been a petri dish for iterating on methods of productive disagreement. I've spent the last few years conducting experiments, both online and in person, to test theories about our existing habits regarding bias and communication, as well as better strategies for managing those biases. This research has persuaded me that the art of productive disagreement is *the most important metaskill anyone can acquire.*

I've become much more concerned when I see people being too polite and conflict *avoidant* than when conflict is surfacing and be-ing heard. Hidden disagreements are much worse than surfaced disagreements. Kim Scott, the author of *Radical Candor,* calls this impulse toward kindness "ruinous empathy" because it actually causes more problems than it solves. It's a real thing that has begun to take hold in our companies, at our dinner tables, and even in our own heads. It happens when people care a lot about things, but for cultural or personality-based reasons, they feel it is best not to challenge them directly.

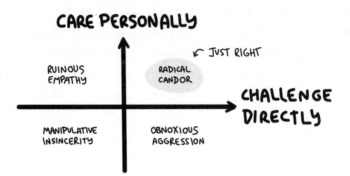

Disagreements are a sign of group health, not pathology, and cultures that allow the airing of grievances in a way that addresses them productively are more likely to create successful relationships, businesses, and communities.

Surprising truth: people are happier, and groups are higher-functioning, when the flow of necessary disagreements is open and they have an honest chance to be heard.

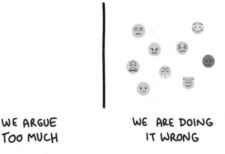

Are all arguments the same? Certainly not. We're going to take apart arguments as if we were dissecting a frog to find out what's inside. We can't unilaterally state that all arguments are bad any more than we can say that all frogs have brown eyes. Brown might be the most common color, but that statement hides a surprising amount of variety while simultaneously discouraging closer inspection.

Fun fact: Frogs' eyes come in a variety of colors from red, orange, and yellow to copper, silver, bronze, and gold. In most frogs and toads the pupil is horizontal, but some pupils are vertical, and some varieties of frogs have pupils that are round, triangular, heart shaped, hourglass shaped, or diamond shaped. When you unblind the stereotype around frogs' eyes, you find all kinds of fantastic diversity. The same is true of arguments.

If we unfold our one-dimensional understanding, we'll see that a simple generalization like "arguments are good" or "arguments are bad" won't suffice for the same reason: it obscures the surprising variety of arguments that closer inspection reveals. Let's begin by categorizing arguments as productive or unproductive. If we get into an argument and come away with a better understanding of what's going on or a better plan for what to do next, that not only cancels out the negative emotions but turns them into positive ones!

With these categories, we can ask better questions. What makes arguments productive? How can I make my arguments more productive? As we would with any work of art, we can study our subjects with curiosity, and learn to see them in new ways. Let's start simply, by unlearning some things about yelling.

MISCONCEPTION 2

Arguments Change Minds

We can really change only two things: our own minds and our own behavior.

What is a disagreement? In the simplest terms, let's say that it's *an unacceptable difference between two perspectives.* They appear in every corner of our lives, not to mention also under our rugs and in our closets.

EXAMPLES FROM EVERYDAY LIFE:

Someone swoops in and takes the parking spot you were patiently waiting for.

You accidentally sleep in, and blame your spouse for turning the alarm clock off too soon.

You call a retailer to complain that the pants you just bought tore in an embarrassing way and you want a refund.

EXAMPLES FROM CONVERSATIONS ONLINE:

Your aunt defends a celebrity accused of sexual misconduct, and you think there are too many people speaking out against him for there to be any chance he's innocent.

Your friend's Facebook page blows up in an argument about whether or not wearing a certain hat makes them a racist.

You think the photo being shared around looks like a white dress with gold lace, and others think it looks like a blue dress with black lace.

EXAMPLES FROM MYTHOLOGY AND FICTION:

Sam-I-am is insistent that his grumpy friend try some green eggs and ham, and his friend doesn't want them here or there. He doesn't want them anywhere.

Zeus chains Prometheus to a rock, where every day his liver is eaten by a giant eagle and then grows back again, because he doesn't think Prometheus should have given humans the gift of fire.

Darth Vader wants Luke Skywalker to join him in a quest to end destructive conflict and restore order to the galaxy. Luke declines the offer.

EXAMPLES FROM POLITICS:

You think taxes should be raised on the wealthy, and your parents think there should be a flat tax that's the same for everyone.

You think it's important for everyone to get a free university education, and your senator thinks the federal government should only pay for people who would have qualified for a loan.

You vote for candidate A, because you think they'd be more likely to win the general election, and your friend votes for candidate B, because they think they'd do a better job if elected.

EXAMPLES FROM YOUR INTERNAL MONOLOGUE:

You feel like you shouldn't have that third slice of pizza, but you love cheese so much.

You want a new car, but you also want to have money.

You want it to be sunny, but also like this new scarf you just bought.

IT'S EASY TO SEE HOW we go from different perspectives to the conclusion that the best way to resolve the disagreements is to change someone's mind. If the perspectives didn't disagree anymore, then the disagreement would disappear. So which side wants to volunteer?

The key word in our definition of a disagreement (an unacceptable difference between two perspectives), isn't "difference." It's "unacceptable." Once the clash between perspectives becomes unacceptable, our motivation shifts from understanding minds to changing them, and from that shift springs a world of trouble.

We can change our own beliefs and our own behaviors, but when it comes to changing other people, our options are more limited and the results can vary wildly. Sometimes our attempts to change minds can actually have the opposite effect, making people dig in their heels even deeper in their current belief. It's called the backfire effect.

Trying to persuade people too much can backfire.

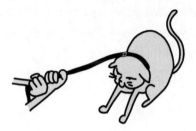

For example:

- You have two good friends who start dating. When they break up, one of the friends asks you to stop being friends with the other. The backfire effect might lead you to actually reach out to the other friend or even to sympathize with them more.

- Your boss tells you that you absolutely have to work weekends and refrain from drinking or smoking in your off hours, in order to be sharp on the job. The backfire effect might lead you to do those things *even more* than you otherwise would.

- Your sibling is a fan of a sports team that's a rival of the one you both grew up supporting. Your sibling's team wins, and he or she rubs it in, saying you should give up being a fan of your team. The backfire effect might lead you to go out and buy extra team swag and make a point to flaunt it next time you see them.

Why does this happen? The common thread among all of these behaviors that show up as a result of the backfire effect is our perception of an unacceptable demand on our freedom. We may or may not have strong beliefs about which friend is to blame for the breakup, or how much we want to indulge in drugs and alcohol on our own time, or which team deserves our loyalty, but we do have strong beliefs about what we think other people should be allowed to request of us. When others infringe on this deep core value, it sparks the backfire effect more than anything else.

The ancient Greek myth of Eris, the goddess of discord, chaos, and misery, shows us how much trouble we can get into when we try to change people's minds.

ERIS

When every other god and goddess on Olympus was invited to the wedding of Theseus and Peleus except for Eris, she was furious. What, they didn't want her to ruin their good times with all of her chaos, misery, and discord? It honestly sounds like a fair enough reason to me, but Eris wasn't having it. "It's not *my* fault that I'm the goddess of discord!" When Zeus refused to change his mind, she decided to show him what chaos, misery, and discord were all about. (Classic backfire effect: Zeus tried to limit Eris's freedom and instead sparked an escalation of the very thing he was trying to prevent. For all their might and power, the Greek gods were terrible at the art of productive disagreement.)

Eris snuck into the wedding festivities and tossed a golden apple into the crowd inscribed with "To the most beautiful." (Now it's Eris's turn to try to change Zeus's mind about never inviting her to a wedding party.)

THE APPLE OF DISCORD

Obviously, every goddess on Olympus wanted to claim the title of most beautiful (because sexist beauty ideals are not a problem the Greek gods have yet solved). Zeus, knowing that this could get messy, remembered the shy shepherd Paris was supposed to be the most fair judge in the land and appointed him to make the call.

There was only one apple, and nobody thought to inscribe a bunch of apples and avoid all this drama, and so a heated disagreement ensued among the goddesses. If the goal was to get Paris's fair and honest opinion, they could have just asked him for it. But no, instead they each invented their biggest and boldest bribe in order to nudge Paris to their side.

Paris, weighing his options, decided that Aphrodite was the most beautiful goddess because she had the best bribe. This is how persuasion works . . . which is very different from the art of productive disagreement. Persuasion is all about piling incentives, rewards, and sometimes threats onto a decision in order to tip the scales in your favor. Aphrodite "won" the debate by promising the heart of Helen of Troy to Paris, but did winning mean she was the most beautiful? It's not clear. In addition, there was also the small matter of causing the Trojan War, which lasted decades and led to the fall of Troy. All that in order to persuade—or, if we rewind further back, all because Eris tried to change Zeus's mind about whether he should invite her to a party. When disagreements stack high enough, you can end up causing quite a bit of damage. At the end of the day, no minds were changed, everything backfired, and Eris's reputation for discord, chaos, and misery was confirmed to everyone in attendance, yet again.

The lesson? When we try to "win" arguments by whatever means are at our disposal, including persuasion, bribery, threats, and other tools of force, we don't end up getting the results we hope for. At best, Aphrodite got the meaningless apple, Eris got revenge, and excess resentment poured below the surface to feed the roots and bulbs of tomorrow's, next month's, and next year's future disagreements.

Changing minds is really hard. There's really only one mind in the universe that you can change, with some luck, and that's yours. Think about the last time you changed your own mind about something: did you do a complete 180, or was it more of a gradual shift?

A mind is more like a pile of millions of little rocks than a single big boulder. To change a mind, we need to carry thousands of little rocks from one pile to another, one at a time. This is because our brains don't know how to rewire a full belief in one big haul. New neuron paths aren't created that quickly. You might be able to get a tiny percent of someone's mind to rewire to a new belief in a given conversation, but minds change slowly and in unpredictable ways. You might be changing it in the wrong direction.

We have a tendency to continue to maintain old perspectives after we've "decided" to change our mind. That's called the continued influence effect, which is one of more than two hundred cognitive biases that subtly influence how we think and that we'll be discussing in much greater detail in chapter 3.

If we can't change minds, at least we can change what people do, right? Changing other people's behavior is possible, especially if you use force. But this too can easily trigger backfire effects that aren't immediately apparent. Will Eris be invited to the next big wedding? Unlikely! Will Aphrodite be declared the most beautiful goddess next time the question comes up? Not unless you want another city to fall. Similarly, when I bribe my son to clean his room with the promise of more screen time, will the virtues of cleanliness and personal responsibility grow in his heart, leading him to clean his room without prompting in the future? Nope. Will employees do better work if you force them to show up at a certain time and to work a certain number of hours? Will loyalty programs in stores make customers more loyal? Will slaps on wrists to corporations who break the law make them more likely to adhere to it next time? No, no, and a big fat no.

Okay then. If we can't change minds and we can't reliably lean on changing behavior either, what other options do we have? The first step is to acknowledge the backfire effect and pay close attention to both the short-term *and* long-term cycles of disagreement to see how they play out in seen and hidden worlds.

THE WEEDS ARE GONE!

If you see patterns like this in your life—problems appear, you whack them, they disappear, and then they somehow magically return again—don't fool yourself into thinking that the weeds are actually gone half the year. They're just hiding underground, regaining strength for next season.

———

THE FOLLOWING SPRING, AS PREDICTED, the man's yard is overcome again with even more weeds. This time, instead of turning down his neighbor's advice, he seeks it out, and she agrees to come over and assess the situation.

First, she says, "Weeds are just plants we've chosen to ban from our yards. If you look at what they're good at, they can actually make the ecosystem of your yard healthier. Instead of trying to kill them, think of them as plants that are *very easy* to keep alive."

The neighbor continues: "We should think of the garden as a living ecosystem that includes and benefits from weeds rather than as something that's healthy only if they're completely eradicated. Even if you don't go after their bulbs, you can pull them out, thank them for their service, and compost their leaves, stems, and flowers so they can feed the other plants in your yard, even in death. They're your cheap topsoil replenishers!"

"Wow, that's dark. But okay." The man pauses a second and then asks, "I'm still not quite sure I agree that a garden *needs* weeds. Having a weedless garden seems pretty great to me—I'd save so much time. Why would anyone ever wish for more weeds?"

"It's not about wishing for more weeds," the neighbor says. "Look at my yard. It has fewer weeds than yours, even though I haven't spent nearly as much time as you pulling weeds out. When I do spend time in the yard, I decide which plants I want to have return next year and which I can dig up entirely to make room for something else. It requires an appreciation and understanding of what's happening underground, even if I can't see it directly. You come out once a year and have a very confrontational couple of weeks with your yard, including gnashing of teeth and fists raised to the heavens and *lots* of profanity."

"I come from a . . . loud family. You should meet my father. Sorry about that."

"No need to apologize. It led to us meeting, didn't it? Anyway, I like to spend a little time all year round in my garden, thinking about weeds, plants, insects, little creatures, and dirt. Even when I can't see the weeds, I know they're still there, hibernating in the soil, and I expect and even welcome them back each spring. It's not a battle, because we're all in this together: weeds, plants, creatures, gardeners, garden, clouds, and stars."

"Pass the pipe; you've sold me!" They laugh, and the neighbor spends a couple of hours in the garden investigating and narrating the grand drama unfolding among plant, dirt, and nature in his own backyard.

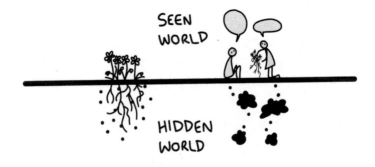

MISCONCEPTION 3

Arguments End

Arguments have deep roots and will always find a way to grow back again.

The story about the weeds isn't entirely fictional. Kellianne and I moved five times during our first six years of marriage, so when we bought a house in Berkeley, California, in 2014, our intention was to put down some roots. Our first son, Niko, was four, and we wanted him to have some stability with schools and friends when the time came.

We didn't realize till the next spring that something else had also decided to take root on our property: a cute little yellow-flowered plant called oxalis, or wood sorrel, or sour grass. I'm pretty sure it's Eris's favorite flower.

NEXT YEAR'S PROBLEMS

The first time we cleared them out we thought we were done with them. But it turns out you're never done with oxalis. Every one you pull out leaves a dozen or more little bulbs waiting to grow into new plants in the future. As new homeowners excited about settling in and working on our yard, those little yellow flowers gave us nightmares. How could we get rid of them? I started seeing them everywhere I went, and I began to judge my neighbors by how many of them they had growing in their yards.

Every relationship is like a garden, and every garden has weeds. Arguments are the little weeds of our relationship that grow up around the things we intentionally plant. Some arguments don't seem so bad and might be easy to work around whenever they pop

up. Others might be ugly enough that you go nuclear on them, and that patch of the yard is abandoned as scorched earth for a couple of years. Either way, the weeds always come back, as reliably as the days and the seasons, despite our attempts to get rid of them once and for all.

This is true not only of the arguments we have but also the ones we don't have.

Arguments don't end, because they have long, long roots. They might disappear from the surface of reality, but they're just hiding.

In a relationship, we have to cobble together compromises at regular intervals to help bridge the gap between our different tastes and preferences. There's probably no effective strategy that can be found to help us permanently "convert" the other person to our tastes and preferences. This is obvious when you actually consider it, but when a disagreement over "What is meaningful to me?" is mistaken for another kind of disagreement, like "What is the right way to balance our preferences?" it can easily get stuck in a bad way. To help us figure out what kind of argument we're having, let's discuss the three realms of disagreement: the head, the heart, and the hands.

THE REALMS OF THE HEAD, HEART, AND HANDS

The easiest thing you can do to have more productive disagreements immediately is to remember to ask the other person: "Is this about what's true, what's meaningful, or what's useful?" Is this about the head, the heart, or the hands? If you can agree on the answer, then you're on your way.

When we're having a disagreement with someone, it's really useful to pay attention to which of the three realms we're experiencing. The three realms are: anxiety about *what is true* (the head realm of information and science), anxiety about *what is meaningful* (the heart realm of preferences and values), and anxiety about *what is useful* (the hands realm of practicality and planning). Each of them represents a part of reality that has its own rules for validation and different implications in a conversation. What works to resolve a disagreement in one realm will not work in the other two.

Head realm: what is true?

When a disagreement can be settled with information, we will call it a conflict of head, because it's about data and evidence that can be objectively verified as true or false out in the world. It is often concerned with the "what" of a situation.

Example: Two people have an argument about who gets to spend more time watching shows that they like versus shows that the other person likes. The resolution to this disagreement is measured in hours, with some bias toward recent days.

♥ *Heart realm: what is meaningful?*

When a disagreement can be settled only as a matter of personal taste, we'll call it a conflict of heart, because it's about preferences and values and judgment calls that can be determined only within oneself. It is often concerned with the "why" of a situation.

Example: Two people have an argument about whether a particular show is worth watching. The resolution to this disagreement is measured by personal taste, ability to relate, and appreciation for different kinds of narratives.

✋ *Hands realm: what is useful?*

When a disagreement can only be settled with some form of test, or by waiting to see how things play out in the future, we'll call that a conflict of hands. It is often concerned with the "how" of a situation.

Example: Two people have an argument about the best way to balance TV time that takes into consideration differences in preferences, differences in show schedules, and differences in personal schedules to be agreeable to both parties. The resolution to this disagreement is measured by its utility in the relationship over time.

What if it's all of the above?

Disagreements always have at least one of these conflicts going on, but some will have a blend of two or all three. When that happens, asking "What is this about?" can help us separate these different arguments and then agree on which one should be addressed first.

Acknowledge the shadow.

There's one more realm to mention. Sometimes we think we're disagreeing with someone and don't realize that we're actually arguing with a shadow projection of our own fears and imaginings—and our worst fears at that. Projections are much harder to have productive disagreements with, because they always live up to our most uncharitable stereotypes of them. They will always act the way we expect them to: as our projection, confirming our most uncharitable stereotypes is their job. The antidote to arguing with a projection is to always know *whom* you're disagreeing with, make sure they're a real human being in the conversation with you, and then actually listen to their argument rather than putting words in their mouth.

When you find yourself arguing with your own shadow, you might as well sit down, because it's going to last a very long time.

KELLIANNE AND I HAVE BEEN in our house for five years now and have definitely reduced the rascally oxalis's claim on our yard, but even more important, I've learned to welcome the oxalis when it appears every spring. It has pretty yellow flowers. Our kids enjoy it because you can also eat it and it doesn't taste too bad. Of course, our instinct is still to immediately yank the plants up on sight, but now this task is done with a begrudging respect for our shared enthusiasm for growing roots in sunny Berkeley. This is an argument in the realm of the hands now, which doesn't have an end so much as an established commitment to an open dialogue that carries us from season to season.

When you learn to appreciate how arguments have deep roots in our relationships with others and ourselves, and how they participate in a cyclical dance, springing up every once in a while, it's possible to appreciate them as partners rather than as enemies. The key is to dance between chaos and order with the rhythm of our relationships, maintaining a healthy balance of each.

THE GIFT OF DISAGREEMENT

Truth 1: Arguments aren't bad. They're signposts to issues that need our attention.

Truth 2: Arguments aren't about changing minds. They are about bringing minds together.

Truth 3: Arguments don't end. They have deep roots and will pop back up again and again, asking us to engage with them.

It's easy to understand why we think of arguments as nuisances, like weeds. We don't have time to deal with this crap! Having a disagreement-free week, or even day, seems like the ultimate joy. Why should we wish for more disagreements?

Done right, arguments are opportunities. A productive disagreement is something you'll look forward to rather than dread. It's one that leads to a mutually beneficial outcome.

A productive disagreement yields fruit: the fruit of *security,* by removing a threat, reducing a risk, resulting in a deal, or concluding with a decision; the fruit of *growth,* by revealing new information about the world or each other that makes us see and understand reality more deeply; the fruit of *connection,* by bringing us together and giving us opportunities to forge trust with one another; and the fruit of *enjoyment,* by teaching us to operate with a collaborative mind-set that emphasizes playfulness, adventure, fun, and sometimes even awe.

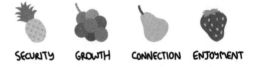

SECURITY   GROWTH   CONNECTION   ENJOYMENT

We've all had good fights, clashes, disagreements—whatever you want to call them—that ended in mutual improvement rather than mutual destruction. They often surprise us, because we didn't expect them to lead to something fruitful. Learning how to increase the chances of this happy surprise is the art we are talking about when we talk about productive disagreement.

This perspective will take time to unfold. But like the neighbor said, it's not a question of wishing for more or fewer disagreements directly, because we don't actually have a choice in the matter. Assuming we're stuck with each other, how can we best get along?

The art of productive disagreement has all kinds of urgent practical applications these days. Our world is becoming increasingly polarized, and even the most chill Zen masters have a limit.

The rest of this book will walk you through the "how" of productive disagreement with eight conversational habits and things to try that will help you turn frustrating battles into pleasant and productive exchanges. I want to emphasize just how much this change will impact your day-to-day life by telling you about three superpowers you will acquire by practicing this art.

1. **Disagreements won't be frustrating.** They'll feel less like dead ends and more like doorways into unexplored territory. You'll learn to identify ways to keep a dialogue open when it seems like you've run out of viable options for moving forward.

2. **You'll end up having fewer repetitive, frustrating disagreements,** not because you're avoiding them or squashing them but because you are able to end the cycles that keep sending the same disagreements back into your life over and over again. You'll learn to pull up disagreements with their roots intact.

3. **The world will become bigger,** because you won't be cut off from all the interesting conversations, ideas, people, and opportunities that exist on the other side of disagreements. You'll find that you've become more

willing to engage with scary people and ideas that you haven't poked with a ten-foot pole in years. You'll learn that opposing perspectives are often quite different when seen from the inside and not nearly as bad as your projection of them from the outside made them look.

YOUR NEW SUPERPOWER

The art of productive disagreement is what some call a metaskill and I call a superpower, because it's a skill that *levels up all of your other skills.*

It's up there with the ability to read or write or think critically. Metaskills are super important to invest in, because if you get marginally better at having more productive disagreements—say, even 5 to 10 percent better—your life could get 50 to 100 percent better! That's because every role you play in your life requires communication and the ability to work through disagreements that pop up. When you learn to disagree productively in different roles, the effects combine and are magnified, making you a better friend, a more competent coworker, a more loving spouse, a more active family member, and a more effective citizen of the world. It's a superpower, because it's probably one of the most high-leverage skills you can work on. Very few people have been given the right tools, rules, and environment to develop and refine their practice of productive disagreement, so we have a lot of room to grow into it.

IF YOU'RE ON THE FENCE

It's quite okay to still be on the fence about productive disagreement. The fence is a safe place to be. You can look around right now, in fact, and see how most of us spend most of our lives on the fence, waiting to figure out what we should do and when we should do it. Cynicism, futility, and frustration aren't pleasant, but they're the devil we know. Before you get too comfortable on the fence, though, let me tell you one more thing that might help nudge you to one side or the other.

The choice you have is not to (a) hide emotions or (b) show them. It's more like the choice Darth Vader gave Luke Skywalker in *Star Wars: Episode V—The Empire Strikes Back*: "We can end this destructive conflict and bring order to the galaxy." It seems tempting, right? Order, in the case of Darth Vader's vision of the Empire, is about establishing an unbreakable power hierarchy that puts the two of them at the top and everyone else below. Hiding emotions might end conflict and bring order, but it does so by pushing below the surface our true selves, which will resurface in the shadowy forms of anxiety, despair, and (if you get mixed up with the dark side) very pale and wrinkly skin. Don't do it! Don't give in to despair. There is a better path that is neither all chaos nor all order—if Dr. Gottman's recipe is on the right track, we could aim for 83 percent order and 17 percent chaos. Relationships and conversations need both order and chaos to be productive.

In a nutshell, balancing order and chaos is what this book will help you get a good start on. At least, this could be the radioactive spider that bites you and recombines your mental DNA to give you this superpower. Designing your costume and coming up with your gimmicky catchphrases are on you.

THE MAP OF ARGUMENTLAND

What does this life of productive disagreement look like? We now move from telling to showing.

In chapter 1 you'll learn to watch how anxiety sparks in your mind, and how this is a signpost pointing to your most important personal beliefs and expectations.

The map will start out fuzzy and become clearer as we go.

In chapter 2 you'll learn how to distinguish between different internal voices that influence your approach to disagreement. We'll use the example of a polarizing issue like the topic of vaccinations to show how it's possible to move from a black-and-white interpretation to one that has a little bit more room for exceptions and gray areas, opening a door for productive one-on-one conversation.

In chapter 3 you'll see how cognitive biases complicate our disagreements and lead to situations where there's no practical way to be completely fair about a decision—for example, a hiring decision—and learn what we can do to reduce the damage of biases in these situations.

In chapter 4 you'll learn how to spot speculation, stereotypes, and oversimplifications masquerading as smart opinions. I share an example from my life of a political conversation with close friends to show how speaking for ourselves, rather than trying to speculate what others think, can make a difference between breaking and building those relationships.

In chapter 5 you'll learn about the power of asking questions that lead to surprising answers. We'll talk about belief in ghosts and the supernatural to show how questions can guide a conversation to new and insightful places that are otherwise missed.

In chapter 6 you'll learn why we need people who disagree with us on our team. I'll share the story of a series of attempts to discuss gun violence and gun control proposals to show how our disagreements become more productive when we build our arguments together.

In chapter 7 you'll learn how the physical space and medium that we have disagreements in impacts the outcome of those disagreements. I'll use this lens to dissect a heated disagreement about immigration enforcement, and you'll learn why it's important to cultivate a neutral space where people are expected and even encouraged to disagree with one another.

And in chapter 8 we'll explore the topic of dangerous ideas. You'll learn why it's important to allow for disagreements about topics that some believe are too dangerous to even talk about.

At the back of the book I've added a bunch of books I recommend for further reading, organized by the chapter they contributed most to.

Like Prometheus's gift of fire, the gift of disagreement is not intrinsically good and must be considered alongside our own value system. The gift of disagreement has never been taught within the context of the kinds of conversations we're having today, so we must also take responsibility for the unintentional damage we cause by participating in and magnifying unproductive disagreements. We can't avoid disagreements any more than we can avoid weeds, and the more we try to eradicate conflict from the world, the more conflict we push into the shadows, where it only grows stronger and returns next season.

THE GIFTS
(AND DOWNSIDES)

OF FIRE — COOK FOOD, WARM HOME, INSPIRE ART, KILL ENEMIES, EXPLORE WILDERNESS, DESTROY TOWNS, PROTECT LOVED ONES

OF DISAGREEMENT — INCITE VIOLENCE, RUIN RELATIONSHIPS, SAVE TIME, INSPIRE ACTION, IS TOO!, IS NOT!, DISCOVER NEW INFORMATION, BURN BRIDGES, BUILD RESPECT

The path forward should be clear. Into the heart of disagreement we must go, with an intention to acknowledge it, appreciate it, and work with it in a way that produces the world we want to live in. I invite you to accept this call to adventure, as a new responsibility required in order for us to meet the new challenges of today.

EIGHT THINGS
TO TRY

YOUR PATH TOWARD THE ART
OF PRODUCTIVE DISAGREEMENT

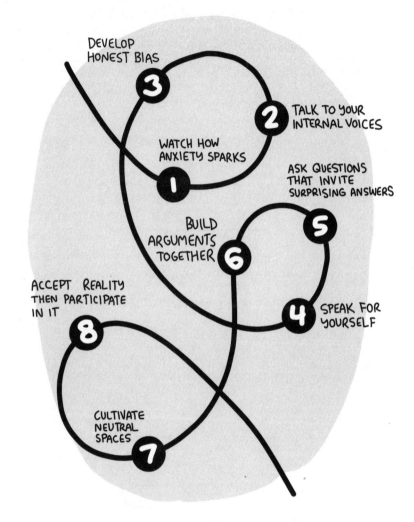

DEVELOP
HONEST BIAS

3

TALK TO YOUR
INTERNAL VOICES

2

WATCH HOW
ANXIETY SPARKS

1

ASK QUESTIONS
THAT INVITE
SURPRISING ANSWERS

5

BUILD
ARGUMENTS
TOGETHER

6

ACCEPT REALITY
THEN PARTICIPATE
IN IT

8

4 SPEAK FOR
YOURSELF

CULTIVATE
NEUTRAL
SPACES

7

1

Watch How Anxiety Sparks

Anxiety is a signpost pointing out
our personal beliefs and expectations.

Has this ever happened to you? You're doing something around the house, and things are a bit chaotic. You grab your lidded coffee cup from earlier in the day off the table and take a big swig. Too late you realize that it must have been an old cup from a week ago that never got thrown away, because you can feel something too horrible to even consider floating in your mouth, and you spit old coffee all over yourself in revulsion. In my defense, this happened to me in college, and I've never looked at an unidentified coffee cup without suspicion since. Experiences, unlike intellectual arguments, can change your mind about something instantly and forever.

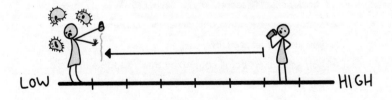

Even if you haven't swallowed moldy coffee, that story probably still sparked some disgust and anxiety in you. Most of us have never received guidance about how to interpret these spikes of anxiety, and thus we often don't remember them or assign meaning to them. But we should, because these sparks are the blazing signposts that tell us that something important to us feels threatened. These signposts are unique to our personal histories and, as a whole, represent a map of our personal expectations, hopes, dreams, and disappointments about the world.

COMMON ANXIETY TRIGGERS

EXPECTATIONS VS REALITY

THAT MUST BE TRUE!   I WAS RIGHT!   THAT CAN'T BE TRUE!

Expectations fall short of reality when:

- Someone says they hate a movie/book/song that you love.
- You put a ton of effort into something that ends up flopping.
- You learn that you're the last person to find out about a shocking family secret.
- Some of your foundational beliefs are challenged in a way you aren't prepared for.
- You get caught doing something that you thought you'd get away with.
- You can't find a way out of an awkward social situation.

Left unquestioned, each of these sparks of anxiety will dictate how we respond to the world like an invisible program: we'll misread people, we'll react incorrectly to new information, and we'll try to force the world to change to meet our expectations rather than update our expectations to better fit the world. Given how little we know and how big the world is, this is almost always a recipe for more anxiety and, ultimately, failure.

AN OLD GLASS OF WATER

One of the first surveys I ran when I was beginning the research that eventually led to this book (and a question I still like to ask people at parties) was about collecting a list of long-running arguments that people have gotten into over and over again. I was looking for the gnarly, twisty, recurring, never-ending arguments, the ones that people repeatedly fell into over the span of years—sometimes decades! These repeating arguments could be with significant others, family members, friends, or just random strangers on the internet. I was especially interested in the ones that seem pretty trivial on the surface but keep coming back again, because something about them taps into deeper emotions and parts of our beliefs and identities. I had a hunch then, and have since confirmed, that arguments live long lives in our heads. Sometimes they stick around for our whole lives, and we practice and refine them with different people at different times. Others are linked to specific relationships, especially with siblings and parents and spouses, and certain topics and perspectives become landmarks to return to over time in these interactions.

One of my favorite arguments came from two good friends of mine, Sharon and Ian. They've been married for over ten years and are both lovely, authentic people who are unafraid of tossing around strong opinions. The argument that Sharon shared with me via private message was surprising all the same: "Does water go bad when it sits out for a few days? We've been arguing about this going on about ten years, and still don't agree. PS. Obviously, yes, the water does go bad."

Perhaps because of my old coffee-cup experience from my college days, I had an immediate reaction to this question and emphatically agreed that the water would be completely and unquestionably undrinkable after a few days. Ian, who grew up in Australia and has a more . . . tolerant relationship to germs, scoffed at us and called us derogatory names. To him, this was just more evidence of how much we had been coddled and possibly ruined by our germophobic culture.

I clarified and opened up the question to a broader group of people to see if it would spark conversation.

Question: If you find a glass of water on your bedside table that's been sitting there three full days, are there good reasons NOT to drink it?

The responses came in fast and ranged across the board. Some of the people who believed the water was okay to drink said things like:

You're all part of the reason we're destroying the planet.

I've even been known (because I'm thirsty or because I hate wasting things) to drink bottled water that's been opened, drunk from (some-

times not by me but by one of my kids), and left in my truck for a week. I'll hesitate more the more uncertain I am of the timeline.

Water left out in a home or office just isn't going to be dangerous or growing any bad bacteria (any more than would be growing on some fruit left on the counter).

And then in the hell-no camp:

No one can change my mind about it. If water has been sitting out overnight, I pour it out and get a fresh one. Every time.

I'd choke on all of the dust and particles that have settled in the open glass.

I can always get another one. There is a risk, admittedly very small, of potentially getting sick, so why take the risk, when the act of getting a new glass of water is so little effort?

I am so closed-minded about this it isn't even funny. That water is absolutely stagnant and will kill you within minutes.

The first surprise

I collected a bit more information from each of the people who responded and created this visualization of their responses so we could all look at this important issue together.

Seeing our very visceral reactions and positions in a two-dimensional space helped us appreciate their diversity. It also had the added benefit of making the responses to the question less personal. The little dots on the chart didn't have names or faces attached (mostly because that would have been beyond my skills). When

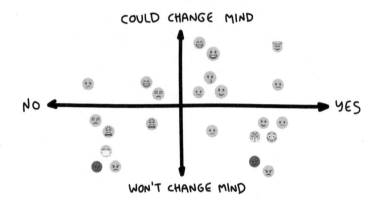

you were looking at the results, it was hard to even remember which dot was your own.

When you depersonalize a position in an argument, it becomes possible to imagine having other positions, in the same way that you might walk around a room and try sitting in different chairs.

The second surprise

The next thing I did was to go back through all the comments people had left and try to cluster reasons people had shared for holding the positions they held. It took a little bit more questioning and back-and-forth, and then some clustering of answers, but fairly quickly I produced a prioritized list of beliefs that each camp used to justify their reactions.

The hell-no camp had a general fear of bacteria and the unknown:

"Nobody knows what's growing in there." People who owned cats had this even more so, because their general assumption was that if a glass of water had been out in their house for more than a couple of minutes, then the cat's dirty paws had gotten in there and filled it with whatever evil germs live in cat poop. That hadn't even occurred to me, since I'm not a cat owner, but it made a lot of sense. Even without cats, I learned that it's true that bacteria will begin to grow in the water, but almost all evidence points to it being generally harmless bacteria.

Another big cluster of responses in the hell-no camp was about taste. Some described the water tasting stale. Others swore that they could taste bacteria and just didn't like that flavor. And a couple of people provided evidence about how water's flavor changes when it gets warmer, and then changes again when the chlorine off-gases. The flavor that some people preferred was most likely a lack of flavor, with a light hint of chlorine. I also learned, in this conversation, that carbon dioxide will dissolve into water that's been left out, and that too has a slight flavor to it.

From the drinkers camp, there seemed to be more personal stories about how respondents overcame their fear of bacteria. These were people who had done a lot of camping, people who grew up in more rural areas of the country or world, people whose parents were doctors and nurses. Here's one of those stories:

My parents were nurses and we have a lot of medical people in my extended family—I think I was raised with the idea that germs and bacteria aren't all bad. Totally ate food off the floor if it fell, got in the dirt a lot, went camping and got dirty a lot, etc. I also don't wear Band-Aids very much, which I never thought was weird until someone pointed it out. Instead I clean a wound with a really strong antiseptic like Hibiclens and let the air take care of it. Maybe just a lot of faith in the body's ability to take care of things? I do wash my hands often because I work with children and grew up watching my parents do it so thoroughly. That said, I'm definitely privileged in that I was blessed with a healthy body and immune system, which is a big part of it. I also have been known to pick up a piece of random food on pretty much any table and pop it in my mouth to see what it is. So half of this reading audience is probably nauseated now.

And finally, there was the person who was the most adamant about not drinking the water, even though she acknowledged that it was probably totally fine. She said:

My strong preference against old water was formed as a young girl just based on taste. Later I formed an actual paranoid delusion about water based on my anxiety disorder. For a time I didn't trust that water was safe to drink if it had been sitting out. When my anxiety got really bad I convinced myself that the water was actually poisoned and would kill me. Now that I've got the anxiety under check, it's a little less nuts, but I still dislike drinking water that's been sitting out. It's mostly taste related but also that I don't want to drink water that has been exposed to dust, pets, and my own mouth bacteria.

We're complicated creatures, and our reactions to things are rooted in long histories and complex emotions. After hearing the variety of stories, and especially this last one, people in the drinkers camp saw the question differently and admitted that personal circumstances inevitably inform our default positions even when they feel purely logical after the fact.

The third surprise

As a first experiment, I felt pretty happy with the results of this survey. I had expected to find a couple of interesting stories, but I also learned some new things about water, bacteria, and flavors along the way. What I hadn't expected was to become curious about what old water tasted like and actually change my preference to drink water from an old glass now and again. When I do, I try to pay attention to the flavors of carbon dioxide, the lack of chlorine, and the faint strains of early bacteria communities sprouting up. I had set up the experiment with a very explicit plea to avoid trying to changing people's minds, and I had marked my own position as fairly unlikely to change based on new information, and yet something had shifted. Did my mind change? Or did my perspective just expand to include a broader set of possibilities?

It didn't do anything to change my skepticism of old cups of coffee, but I have looked at water differently ever since.

FIRST THING TO TRY

Watch how anxiety sparks

Anxiety sparks when a perspective we value bumps into another perspective that challenges it in some way. If we find this new perspective to be unacceptable, that's when our "Someone is wrong on the internet; I must correct them!" impulse leaps into action.

When anxiety sparks—*poof!*—it's like a little anxious dragon is born in our minds, ready to light things on fire. It's the first sign of a disagreement potentially on its way. What else can we notice about this automatic emotional spike? What sparks big anxieties and what sparks little ones?

As we saw in the old-water conversation, the same information (a three-day-old glass of water) can spark a wide variety of anxieties in different people. You can imagine how an early experience like accidentally drinking moldy water, or repeated instances of associating water with poisoning, could magnify the automatic response you'd have the next time, and the next time. Alternatively, growing up in an environment where anxiety was repeatedly reduced by, say, doctor parents or the realities of rural living would result in a completely different response. It's normal to feel the spark of anxiety and immediately assume that it's a reflection of the true qualities of the object we're reacting to. Ivan Pavlov famously showed that dogs could learn to associate dinner with the ringing of a bell until they would salivate when they heard the bell, even before dinner showed up. When we pay attention to the spark of anxiety, we can glimpse how we've learned to react automatically to specific kinds of information. Sometimes, we've learned something that stands up to reflection, like associating gunshots with danger. Other times, we've become conditioned to a belief that doesn't stand up to reflection. We can't know which is which until we look at them.

Let's use a 1 to 5 anxiety-rating scale. We can use it to capture the level of discomfort you experience when you accidentally put something terrible in your mouth and also for the much more general case of expectations and perspectives clashing in your head.

RATE YOUR ANXIETY

Level 1: Pretty manageable. You put on one of your favorite shirts and realize it has a tear in the elbow.

Level 2: You sweat a bit. You hear that your favorite actor committed suicide. You learn that you have a condition that prevents you from eating dairy, gluten, or sugar for the next six months and, depending on the results of the trial period, maybe the rest of your life.

Level 3: There's a mild emergency going on now. Your boss tells you that the business isn't doing as well as hoped and the company has to eliminate some positions, including yours.

Level 4: The problem won't kill you, but you're not going to recover from this unscathed. You learn that your partner cheated on you a few years ago and that it might still be going on. A freak accident kills a close friend.

Level 5: Really bad things happen: you end up in the hospital, a brush fire burns down your block, you lose your spouse or child to a freak accident—you get the point.

Anxiety is subjective. The examples above may even be way off and out of order for you—if so, spend a few minutes calibrating the scale to your own experiences.

You'll also notice that anxiety doesn't have to lead to a disagreement. The kind of anxiety we're discussing is caused by any internal inconsistency between two perspectives. Sometimes one perspective is your beliefs and another is someone else's beliefs; other times one perspective is your expectations about what's real and the other is new information that contradicts those expectations.

Scan this list of potential triggers for anxiety and attempt to rate them 1 to 5 on your own anxiety scale:

You are in a rush to get to work and your main route is unexpectedly under construction, adding an hour to your arrival time.

Your friend throws a plastic bottle into the garbage can, even though there's a recycling bin sitting right next to it.

You learn, as a child, that adults were lying to you about something (Santa, for example) when someone tells you that what you believed isn't true.

Your friend tells you she thinks your house is haunted by the previous owner of the house, who apparently hung herself in the basement. She wants to help you find an exorcist, but they're pretty expensive.

You learn that you were not accepted to the college you wanted to get into, or weren't hired for the job you just interviewed for and really wanted.

Your mom tells you she voted for a different presidential candidate than you did.

You get diagnosed with cancer, and the doctors think you have less than six months to live.

Your favorite television show gets unexpectedly canceled.

Your childhood friend who never went to school or worked a day in his life wins several million dollars in the lottery.

You sense something off in an old, dusty house and hear a voice that sounds like a scream, but you're the only person there.

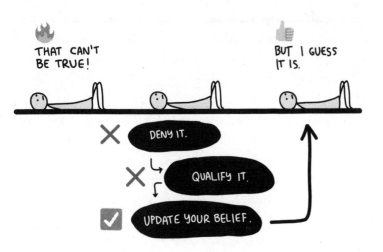

HOW TO STOP ANXIETY
FROM DERAILING YOUR DISAGREEMENT

1. When you notice anxiety, pause and ask yourself: are you anxious about what is true, what is meaningful, or what is useful?

2. Ask the other party the same question. Do they give the same answer or something different?

3. Narrate out loud what each of you is anxious about (this buys more time and slows things down). Reiterate how each of you answered the question to see if that leads to new connections for yourself or the other person.

4. Check to see if either of you is willing to switch to what the other is anxious about. Who has more cognitive dissonance happening and could use the other's help?

Your horoscope tells you that something bad might happen soon, and the next day your car gets a flat tire and you almost crash.

Your friends who you considered to be the perfect happy couple are getting divorced.

You find out the man you thought was your father isn't your biological father.

You get to a friend's house and find them burning a pile of American flags in their fire pit while taking a lot of selfies.

You learn that most parents in your kid's elementary school don't vaccinate their children.

You are at a restaurant with a communal table and realize, after an hour of pleasant conversation, that the party of ten people next to you are all registered sex offenders.

You're camping deep in the forest and wake up feeling a little itchy, but it's pitch-black outside. You turn on a flashlight and realize you and your entire tent are covered in ants.

CAN A BAGEL BE TRIGGERING?

Once you start noticing how anxiety sparks, you'll see it happen everywhere. What's your first reaction when you see bagels sliced vertically, like a loaf of bread?

If your response is anything like the responses that I saw when this was posted on Twitter, you're probably feeling something like level 2 or even level 3 anxiety. The responses on Twitter were entertaining:

Officer, I would like to report a crime.
First of all, how dare you
Who told you this was ok

It's not unusual to routinely feel anxious when other people do completely harmless things that don't align with our preferences.

The bagel meme trended on Twitter for a day or two, and it's a good example of why the internet is fun: we're playing social games that help us reduce shared anxieties, even silly ones, while at the same time pouring our other anxieties into the platform.

The setup of any joke, story, or headline in the news requires the creation of anxiety. Anxiety, in fast-moving formats like these, is highly motivating. The psychological term for this is cognitive dissonance, and every time we experience cognitive dissonance, we are motivated to Whac-A-Mole it (or "reduce it," if you're using the official words). Think about it: every single performer, publisher, comedian, product, service, business, advertiser, or other entity that wants your attention for marketing purposes, entertainment purposes, or more nefarious purposes uses ideas that generate cognitive dissonance as a way to grab your attention. If they can make you feel tense, then you're more likely to pay attention to whatever they point to for resolution.

Social media helps with shared anxiety reduction because we ca band together in either *qualifying* a conflicting perspective ("The aren't real bagels"; "This is a St. Louis thing, and they're weird") *rejecting* a conflicting perspective ("If you slice a bagel like it's a lo of bread you deserve life in prison. No exceptions"). The downsi of this fast, reactive social game is that we become dependent social media to resolve our anxiety, and we don't get as much pra tice resolving it on our own. If social media makes you anxiou this might be part of the reason why.

Depending on which social game we use to reduce cognitive d sonance in ourselves, we may end up with less charitable and l accurate understandings of other people. Recall that a disagreem can be about what is true, what is meaningful, or what is usef Your job is to identify which type or types of disagreements y want to have. Maybe you want to focus on whether it's *meaningfu* slice a bagel only a certain way. Maybe someone else wants to fo on whether it's *useful* to slice a bagel only a certain way. If w talking about personal preferences and values, we should confi that this is what others are talking about too before making a case what we prefer. Questions about cultural context, tradition, and cumstances will become relevant. Similarly, if we're talking ab the utility of different methods, then we should confirm that otl are on the same page with us on that, because it leads to questi like "What is this method useful for?" and "What goals are volved?" Each realm of disagreement is a different world of inve gation with different ways to validate or resolve perspectives. W anxiety sparks a disagreement, and you not only notice it but rate it on a 1 to 5 scale, you're at a fork in the road, and the way choose to reduce cognitive dissonance will play a giant role in l productive the next few minutes will be. Even if you start in der you can slowly work through qualification and maybe even up ing if you allow yourself to dwell in the dissonance a little longe

If you both settle on a question about what is true, you can ask:

- Is there a source of information we both trust that could give us the answer to this question?
- What qualifies as a trustworthy source?

If you both settle on a question about what is meaningful, you can ask:

- Why is this important to us?
- What past experiences led to us having these preferences or values?

If you both settle on a question about what is useful, you can ask:

- What would happen if we didn't do anything?
- How confident are we in the outcome of these different proposed actions?

The other thing to be mindful of is the level of anxiety, or cognitive dissonance, in the room (even if it's a virtual room). The amount of cognitive dissonance different people experience will vary depending on how much their in-group identifies with being picky about bagels. New Yorkers might be so anxious about the prospect of "bastardizing" a bagel that they're immediately triggered when that preference is violated. People in groups who are neutral about bagels (of which I'd consider myself a part) might not feel much cognitive dissonance at all. People who are familiar with bread-sliced bagels already (like St. Louis residents) won't feel as much because mere-exposure effect (we tend to prefer things that we have become familiar with) has already reduced their dissonance there.

A third way to reduce cognitive dissonance beyond qualifying or rejecting the conflicting perspective is to *update your perspective* with the new information. A reaction of "bread-sliced bagels is a different way to cut bagels that some people do" is less commonly adapted into social games, because it doesn't have as good a punch line.

When I saw the bagel tweet, my first reaction was rejection ("No way; that's so wrong!"). I favorited a few funny tweets but didn't tweet anything myself. The next time it popped up, I began to understand that this was happening specifically in St. Louis, a detail I had missed in my first pass. I was reminded of a similarly weird trend in Seattle, wherein hot dog vendors had begun putting cream cheese on hot dogs, and how much I enjoyed that at the end of a night out. This didn't make me want a bread-sliced bagel, but it did make me see that strange local trends happen that seem weird from the outside. This tiny bit of empathy gave me a path to qualifying my belief—I accepted that it's probably okay with me if people want to slice bagels this way—and eventually updating my belief to allow difference on its own merits. ("It's a big world.") This is one way to reduce cognitive dissonance internally—but it also feels weird to have to approve of how other people do things that are completely harmless, doesn't it?

My reaction is partially a function of the level of anxiety I initially felt. I'm not a New Yorker and am not even a very strong bagel enthusiast, so I didn't have to do a lot of work to resolve the anxiety. When dissonance is low, the question of "What is useful?" might be enough to resolve it without additional help. When dissonance is high, it might not be enough, which means people who disagree will need to keep looking for another way to resolve the anxiety.

Jokes and social games are great for off-loading the work of high-anxiety cognitive dissonance. Unfortunately, ridicule, insults, and denial also reduce cognitive dissonance in the moment. Collectively, these are strategies that entangle us and make us dependent on the very communication platforms that caused the anxiety in the first place. This entanglement may have a hand in explaining how meme culture has sprung up so quickly on these platforms. If everyone is using these networks to reduce anxiety while also increasing their chances of being exposed to it, a positive feedback loop of growth begins to develop.

Now that we have a language for talking about the levels of anxiety (1 to 5) and the types of anxiety (head, heart, or hands), we can begin to disentangle ourselves from relying too much on the tools that create cognitive dissonance to also resolve it.

START WITH THE SPARK

My wife, Kellianne, informed me about a school holiday coming up that we hadn't added to our calendar, which meant Niko would be home for the day unexpectedly. I had planned to work as usual, and Kellianne had some important errands to run, so she asked me if I could hang with Niko that morning and head in a couple of hours late. I mentioned, perhaps too nonchalantly, that it would probably be fine to let Niko stay home alone for that time; he's a pretty responsible kid. In the way that these things sometimes happen, this sparked an argument about whether or not it's legal to leave an eight-year-old home alone.

If I had been watching how anxiety sparks, I would have noticed that I had level 1 or 2 anxiety around the possibility of not being able to work that day. My response was to deny that possibility and to reach for the easiest solution to the problem: let Niko stay home by himself. Problem: solved (for me).

Except it wasn't solved for Kellianne. Instead of being resolved, the disagreement only escalated.

KELLIANNE: We can't do that! That's against the law, and I don't feel comfortable leaving him home by himself. What if something happened? We'd have no way of knowing.

IS LEAVING KIDS AT HOME AGAINST THE LAW?

NO — YES

If I had been watching how anxiety sparks, I would have noticed here that my strategy for reducing anxiety didn't work for Kellianne, which should have been enough to make me realize that she'd need another answer. This makes sense, because the source of my anxiety was that I was worried that I wouldn't be able to work, and that was unlikely to be the cause of Kellianne's anxiety. I could have asked at this point what she was worried about, to get a better sense of the disagreement's real source. At the very least I could have dropped the proposed solution that worked only for me and kept looking for one that worked for both of us. Instead, I chose to start a new disagreement about whether or not my solution was legal in California, blindly hoping that that was what she was actually worried about.

> **ME:** I'm pretty sure it's not illegal.
> **KELLIANNE:** No. It's not negotiable. I just don't feel safe.
>   I don't see why you can't just stay home an extra hour.
>   I have been on kid duty every sick day ever, and you
>   never have.
> **ME:** I can stay home for it, but I just think Niko could also
>   handle being alone for an hour or two. He's a responsible kid.

Because I wasn't paying attention to the source of my anxiety, I couldn't see that it was different from Kellianne's source. Therefore, I couldn't see how my solution didn't resolve her problem.

Worst of all, I was insisting on having a disagreement that she didn't actually care about while ignoring the one that she actually wanted to discuss.

If I had been paying better attention to all of this, I would have very easily noticed that for Kellianne, our disagreement had nothing to do with California laws or even with the possibility of leaving Niko at home alone. For her, the disagreement was actually about a value judgment of my willingness to pitch in for the family. By the time this became clear to me (it took a bit longer than it should have), my offer to stay home was no longer enough to salvage the conversation, because it had shifted to a much broader disagreement about my general behavioral trends and even my inability to communicate effectively.

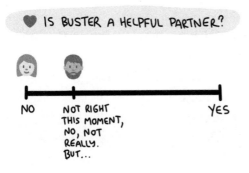

When one person is trying to manage a large source of anxiety, and the conversation focuses on strategies that aren't sufficient to resolve that anxiety, the disagreement will escalate and escalate until a solution that's sufficient appears. Recruiting past disagreements and comparisons to other people and reaching for less healthy methods of resolution like yelling, insults, resentment, and denial become increasingly necessary methods of anxiety management.

This embarrassing personal example points to one of the most common errors made by people who are particularly drawn to "reasonable" debate. People who value cool rationality make this mistake all the time—we focus on arguments in their simplest form (what is true?) when all the emotional evidence is screaming that it's really an argument much more rooted in meaning, value, and/or purpose. Disagreements about information are by far the simplest conflicts to resolve, because there's a source of truth out there, somewhere within reach. All we have to do is reach for it—problem solved. But this easy answer applies only to easy questions, and overrelying on it makes us blind to other more ambiguous and messy parts of relationships that aren't as easily addressed. Many more arguments than we're usually willing to admit are about personal preferences (why was I putting work above family?) and/or about strategy and pragmatism (was leaving Niko home alone the best option in this particular situation?). By holding on to the easy, information-based conflict, I exacerbated the other two kinds of conflict. I believed that I always try to put family above work and that I was willing to stay home during Kellianne's errands . . . but I was proving with my actions that this wasn't in fact true.

Instead of reaching for the easy but misguided disagreement, I should have asked myself, "Is it possible that I'm not contributing enough to our family?" Yes, it's definitely possible. "Is it possible that Niko isn't quite ready to stay home by himself?" Also definitely possible. "Given these possibilities, what questions could I ask and what things could I do to more conclusively eliminate them as possibilities?" These questions were my takeaways from the conflict retrospective that I held in my own head, a day later, and they led to follow-ups and brainstorming with Kellianne over the subsequent weeks.

Asking those questions wasn't natural in the moment and continues to be something that I practice in many of my conversations. The key to beginning to shift these deeply wired conversational habits that we've picked up over the course of our lives is to start with the spark.

Talk to Your Internal Voices

They represent the default reactions
to anxiety that we've inherited from
our parents and broader culture.

et's say that you are super pro-vaccination and believe that everyone should be vaccinated, full stop. When you believe this and come into contact with people who are anti-vaccination, it's likely that you experience some anxiety—maybe a lot. Let's represent it like this.

This is one way to visualize cognitive dissonance. The further the conflicting perspective is from your own, the larger the cognitive dissonance. The amount of anxiety we feel about a position impacts our impression of the person holding the view that caused it. In discussing highly polarizing issues, we will sometimes demonize people who claim to hold a view that we believe is truly unacceptable.

It works both ways, of course. The nature of polarization requires both sides to hold strong opinions about the unacceptability of the other's stance. Here's how someone who believes vaccinations are potentially harmful might feel about this issue (essentially a mirror of the above).

The goal here is to visualize the cognitive dissonance from both sides, *even if you don't believe both sides are reasonable*. This distinction is important. We all have our own positions on these issues and usually believe that one side is more valid than the other, and there's plenty of time to tear an argument down. Before you do that, however, it helps if you first understand it. Visualizing it helps.

This first step of acknowledging the "inside view" of the other side's beliefs is designed to make sure that we don't jump too quickly to demonization. At what point do you lose empathy for the other side? And how well do we understand how the other side sees us? The key to not demonizing the other side too hastily is to understand where the automatic tendency to demonize others is coming from—our internal voices—and to double-check with these internal voices that their stereotypes are accurate.

Eve Pearlman, journalist and CEO of Spaceship Media, a new company dedicated to encouraging what she calls "dialogue journalism," has been running experiments on Facebook and in the real world bringing together people on two sides of a polarized issue. In one of the first experiments, she brought twenty-five people who had voted for Donald Trump and twenty-five people who had voted for Hillary Clinton into a Facebook group that lasted a month. She started the conversation by asking both sides to describe how they thought the other side saw them. The people who voted for Trump said that they thought the Clinton voters saw them as "religious Bible thumpers" who are "backwards, hickish, and stupid." Meanwhile, the people who voted for Clinton said that they thought the Trump voters saw them as "crazy, liberal Californians, unpatriotic, wealthy, and putting career over family."

When both sides think the other side demonizes them, it justifies demonizing them back. This perspective leverages this demonization in order to justify force that might otherwise be questionable. In Eve's experiment, those flat, angry, mean caricatures were dismantled by being exposed. Both sides could see that the other wasn't quite as flat, angry, and mean as they were expecting them to be, and this meant demonization couldn't take over.

Unfair caricatures are just one of the side effects of what psychologist and economist Daniel Kahneman calls "System 1"—the fast, instinctive, emotional system of our brain that tries to make most of our decisions while requiring the least amount of energy. This system relies on habits of thought and quick, reliable shortcut strategies to get things done. It stands in contrast to System 2—the slow, more deliberative, more logical thinking system that takes a lot of energy and is what we typically think of as conscious thinking.

You won't be surprised to hear that anxiety shapes the recommendations made by our fast, cheap, instinctual System 1. In the case of a pro-vaccination person hearing about an outbreak of measles in an affluent American town because of low vaccination rates, the recommendation from System 1 might be "Keep them as far from my family as possible, and make vaccinations mandatory!" If a pro-vaccination person accuses an anti-vaccination person of killing children, the anti-vaccination person's System 1 might recommend that they flee to avoid harsh accusations that they don't feel they deserve. These internal voices rise up quickly; that's how System 1 works. Our internal voices are automatic, filled with emotional and urgent declarations often related to safety. They make use of stereotypes and group labels to categorize threats and opportunities and our relation to them. They are blind to the passage of time—everything happening now has always happened and will always happen, unless drastic measures are taken. They are sensitive to power dynamics and will employ fight-or-flight solutions depending on one's relationship to the threat. Bosses will yell and attack. Employees will flee for cover. Parents will take away toys. Children will cry.

And yet, with practice, we can learn to step back, listen to System 1, and take its messages more as suggestions rather than orders. If we pay more attention to how we talk to ourselves, we'll see that the thoughts and feelings that flow naturally from the spark of anxiety are only our internal voices and not the final say on what we absolutely need to think and feel.

FOUR INTERNAL VOICES

Putting a face on System 1

Broadly speaking, we have four internal voices spewing automatic thoughts and suggesting conflict modes to us. Each of us has some version of these preprogrammed voices in our heads, but the descriptions here are entirely unscientific, and you should interpret them only as cookie-cutter templates that make it easier for us to talk about them. They've been installed by our culture, our parents, our community, and our experiences.

The four voices I'd like to call out are the voice of power, the voice of reason, the voice of avoidance, and the voice of possibility. They speak up especially loudly when there's a spark of anxiety and cognitive dissonance happening, because they exist to help us reduce our anxiety, one way or another.

THE VOICE OF POWER

"Might is right." "Take it or leave it." "My way or the highway." "Do as I say." "That's an order!" "This isn't a debate!" "Beggars can't be choosers." "Finders keepers, losers weepers."

The voice of power is the most primal and ancient voice in our head. It resolves disagreements by forcefully shutting them down. It's the one that is *so done* talking and is willing to play the bad cop if it needs to. If the disagreement is about who gets something, the voice of power will claim "Mine!" and yank it out of the other person's hand. If that doesn't work, it'll try biting and clawing and whatever other tactics are available to it.

Cultural references that help implant this voice in us include:

- The belief that strength and power are evolutionary advantages
- Sun Tzu's *The Art of War* and military strategy in general
- A common refrain in Silicon Valley: "Fake it till you make it."
- Nike's slogan "Just do it!"
- Gunboat diplomacy, a policy under which nineteenth-century imperial powers used displays of strength to intimidate less powerful states to concede power to them. This strategy is embodied by Theodore Roosevelt's famous quotation "Speak softly and carry a big stick and you will go far."
- "Woe to the conquered!"

My younger son, Louie, had a favorite toy when he was about two years old—it was a pink train named Rosie. He sometimes woke up in the morning and, before doing anything else, screamed "PINK CHOO CHOO TRAIN!" across the house. That was our cue, as his parents, to try to remember where we last saw this train and to deliver it to him before he decided he needed to escalate the incident to the next level (which would involve kicking the wall and shaking the whole house). There's no doubt in my mind that we're born with the voice of power in our heads from day one;

there's no room for subtlety when you're a newborn or toddler with needs. Of course, for Louie, this voice hadn't yet been calibrated to be used only for severe threats and so would be used even when his best friend—let's call her Ellie—joined us for lunch at a local café and accidentally started playing with the train he had brought along.

LOUIE: MY TRAIN!

Ellie, being two herself and also unaware of the level 5 anxiety Louie was experiencing, but very aware of her own level 5 anxiety created by the sudden yelling, said, "NO, MY TRAIN!"

Louie attempted to forcefully grab the train out of Ellie's tightening grasp. Ellie screamed and swatted him away. One parenting strategy available to me as I witnessed this scene was to make sure real harm didn't happen but to otherwise let them sort it out. But of course all of this sparked some anxiety in me as well. I had enough of my mental capacity functioning to see that I too had a voice of power in my ear telling me to yell at them and order them to shut up. But it wasn't the only voice. In fact, another voice exists to specifically keep the voice of power in check: the voice of reason, which we'll get to next.

The voice of power is the ultimate conflict-resolution strategy, because you can't argue with sheer force. That's what power does—it forcibly closes down arguments and ends conflict in your favor, which is an undeniable evolutionary advantage.

The voice of power is useful beyond one-on-one combat as well. Totalitarian dictatorships use this strategy to rule, silencing and even killing dissenters. Revolutions use the voice of power to eventually overthrow those dictators and start anew. The only downside of the voice of power is that a battle must occur, which potentially damages both sides. So while it's the oldest known strategy to resolve pretty much any disagreement imaginable, it's also the most expensive. It's not sustainable without significant turnover if those in power are expected to fight every challenger—which opens the possibility for the voice of reason to bring efficiency and calculation to the table.

Whenever you hear yourself or someone else say, "This conversation is over!" "We're done here!" or just a flat "No means no!" and the speaker is in a position to enforce that declaration, they're using the voice of power. Whenever we resort to blocking, censoring, or exiling people or their dangerous ideas, we're exercising the voice of power. There's undeniable satisfaction in these moves, of course, as well as immediate benefits from shutting down an unproductive conflict with a ruling in your favor, but there are also downsides.

THE VOICE OF REASON

"Why?" "Show me the evidence." "Prove it."
"That doesn't add up." "What's fair is fair."
"I didn't make the rules." "That's not how
it's done."

The voice of reason is all about using, well, *reasons* to shut down a debate. A reason could be as simple as the threat of force but is usually attributed to some higher authority than just raw strength: the greater good, common sense, tradition or convention, etc. The voice of reason is an upgrade over the voice of power because it can win without a fight—though it's not guaranteed to work on someone who's deploying the voice of power.

The fable about the hawk and the nightingale demonstrates this principle well. The story goes something like this:

A hawk seizes a singing, and much smaller, nightingale. Upon capture, the nightingale cries out in protest. The hawk says, "Miserable thing, why do you cry? I'm much stronger than you, and I'll eat you if I feel like it." The hawk is the voice of power incarnate.

The nightingale, lacking power, resorts to reason and pleads with the hawk: "But wait! I'm way too small to satisfy the hunger of a hawk like you. How about this—you let me go and I will sing a beautiful song for you and it will make you happy. Then you can go eat one of those larger birds over there!"

Hawk: "Interesting offer. However, I prefer that you soothe my stomach."

The moral of the story is: a hungry stomach has no ears, even for the beautiful song of a nightingale. How does the voice of reason get around this problem? Simple: with numbers.

Birds like the nightingale survive to this day because they do have a viable defense against hawks: they participate in a social activity called mobbing. If a hawk swoops into their territory, the first one to spot it will cry out with a mobbing call, which is essentially an alarm bell to warn the other birds of the danger. The birds will then collectively swarm around the predator and force it to leave because, united, they are more powerful than the hawk.

The voice of reason is built on top of the voice of power, as an enhancement more than anything else. Once it is established in a position of power, the voice of reason can then establish a higher *authority* (for example, a religious or legal system) to maintain that power without having to pay the more expensive costs of constant battling that the voice of power must do. The higher authority of reason does two things at once: it keeps the group together, because the group is what protects it from outside threats, and it resolves disputes internally in a way that doesn't harm the group.

Institutions that make use of the voice of reason as an enhancement on top of the voice of power include:

- **Religion:** A system of belief that includes faithful membership as a criterion for spiritual reward. May resort to violent extremism if reason fails.
- **Democracy:** A system of government wherein citizens exercise power by voting and benefit from an agreement to follow the rules of citizenship. May resort to revolution if reason fails.
- **Capitalism:** An economic and political system wherein everything is traded for money and valued by its price. May resort to sanctions, buyouts, lobbying, blackmail, and bribery if reason fails.
- **Science:** A body of knowledge and meaning acquired through observation, experimentation, and replicability. May resort to technological and/or economic warfare if reason fails (perhaps the least scary of the bunch, but maybe the most effective).

What these institutions all have in common is an internal system of reason constructed on top of a system of power. They're each complete with foundational beliefs and trickle-down assumptions about what's reasonable and what's not. These systems seem self-evident and internally consistent to their followers. What passes as reasonable and acceptable, however, will differ from institution to institution. A perfectly reasonable statement made within an institution of science can appear very unreasonable to someone who belongs to an institution of religion or even a different institution of science.

In exchange for adhering to their internal system of reason, institutions offer protection to members of the group in the form of tools and incentives for coordinating with other members of the group. When addressing conflict using the voice of reason, the greatest crime is to betray the group and the ultimate punishment is to be exiled from the group. For example, if a business disagrees with its tax rate and refuses to pay its taxes to the government, it will not be in business for long. If a Catholic bishop refuses to recognize the authority of the pope, he won't be a bishop for long. If an employee decides that they disagree with their work hours, they won't have a job for long.

The dynamic that reinforces the power of the voice of reason within the group also presents its greatest flaw: each of these institutions must adopt different strategies for resolving disagreements *within* their institution than they use when resolving disagreements *across* institutions. Institutions of reason aren't well equipped to have productive disagreements with other institutions that don't respect their primary system of authority. Institutions also can't use their greatest punishment of exile to influence people outside the group, because those people aren't members in the first place.

The voice of reason shines when it speaks to people who belong within the same group.

When Louie and Ellie were fighting over the pink train, the voice of reason could appeal to the higher authorities of the shared community that we all belonged to. These higher authorities feel like cultural norms and "good behavior" to everyone inside the group.

As I witnessed this scene unfolding, the voice of reason suggested each of these cultural norms to me as ways to intervene and settle the dispute:

- Sharing
- Taking turns
- Finding something else to play with
- Not yelling
- Not hitting

ME: Louie, can you be nice and share your train with Ellie?
LOUIE: NO!

Okay, that didn't work. Next, I surveyed the room and looked for more trains and other toys that I might be able to persuade Louie to play with instead until Ellie got bored of the train, in thirty seconds or less. But this was the pink train. *The* pink train. So that wasn't going to work. It was irreplaceable to Louie. But how about Ellie—what could I bribe her with? I knew she loved strawberries. Putting on my cheery parental host voice, I announced, "Oh, look, I have some strawberries over here. Ellie, do you want one?"

ELLIE: Yes.

Louie, perhaps wondering why Ellie was being given strawberries and he wasn't, suddenly valued the urgent playdate with his train a bit less than before. While they ate strawberries, I snuck the pink train away.

If other people were watching this scene, they would probably react with something between annoyance and bemusement, depending on whether their particular learned expectations for appropriate conduct in a café leaned more toward being child-free or child-friendly. However, imagine the reaction if, instead of offering strawberries to children under my care, I went and offered strawberries to the children of strangers without their permission. That might trigger entirely different norms that would put me outside the bounds of acceptable behavior. Now, imagine if I brought strawberries to a board meeting in an attempt to get people to stop arguing about a serious business objective. The voice of reason operates within the group dynamics and cultural norms of the participants, and it completely falls apart when trying to address problems outside of that group's most prevalent cultural norms.

The interventions that the voice of reason will suggest in a high-stakes board meeting might look more like this:

- Agreeing to run a test to validate (or invalidate) one of the suggested solutions
- An appeal to authority that allows a mutually respected decision maker to make the call, or an action item to follow up with a recommendation after the meeting
- A compromise allowing one of the parties to disagree and commit, choosing to safely register an opposing opinion without slowing down the momentum of a project

Though these interventions diverge from the doling out of strawberries, they appeal to the same underlying norms of sharing, taking turns, and escalation that children in a café are held to.

The upside of the voice of reason is that when we share cultural norms and respect the same higher authority, we have lots of great tools for resolving differences of perspective in a nonviolent way. The downside is that as culture changes, and as groups grow or shrink or otherwise evolve, cultural norms that used to have wide acceptance fall out of favor and become less useful. For example, not too long ago it was acceptable for parents to spank their children, even in public, when they misbehaved, and it was acceptable for rampant misogyny to go unchecked within corporations.

If in the café I had resorted to spanking instead of strawberries, I would have gotten very different responses from bystanders than I did. Similarly, what is acceptable in a professional environment is no longer driven by a single shared consensus, and a lot of debate is happening around establishing healthier cultural norms regarding what we believe is acceptable and unacceptable, even if it means recasting past behavior as clearly over the line. As our world becomes more blended in terms of cultural traditions and norms, and gives voice to previously disenfranchised demographics, increasingly we can't assume that everyone around us thinks that our norms are normal. What a reasonable person considers acceptable is a moving target, and we all have to be okay with redefining these boundaries, but this fact also reveals that the boundaries are drawn by consensus and not according to any absolute sense of universal morality.

There is not a single objective authority that *all* voices of reason can speak to. You can't use courtroom norms to resolve a disagreement in a relationship any more than you can use scientific studies to resolve a disagreement about your life's purpose. When we try to apply reason across the boundaries of groups with clashing norms, we set ourselves up for a whole lot of yelling and frustration, often leaving us with feelings of futility.

The takeaway here is that the voice of reason relies on having the voice of power to fall back on during escalations, and is best suited to disagreements with people who share respect for the higher authority, and are members of the same groups and institutions, that your reasons draw from. If the voice of reason isn't working, check which groups you both identify with to confirm that the cognitive dissonance you're addressing is a concern for at least one group that you both belong to.

This brings us to the third voice, the voice of avoidance, to which we are increasingly drawn in these polarized times. When power and reason don't work, sometimes the only recourse is to avoid the conversation altogether.

THE VOICE OF AVOIDANCE

"The only winning move is not to play."
"I would prefer not to." "Leave me out of it."

When I share my fascination with arguments and disagreement with people, one of the most common responses I get is that they prefer to avoid arguments whenever possible. If you relate, you are not alone. In fact, you are likely a member of a quiet majority—often also known as the way of the conflict avoider. That term may have positive or negative connotations for you, but for now, let's talk about it as a neutral description of a quiet but effective strategy that we all employ to a certain extent.

Conflict avoiders have identified flaws in the voices of power and reason and so have chosen to address conflicts by simply refusing to participate in them in the first place. "Let others fight if they want to, but as for me, no thanks!" You see someone being unprofessional at work but don't say anything. You dislike the way your partner folds the towels but don't say anything. Your racist relative speaks up at the holiday dinner, but rather than shut him up or attempt to reason with him, you pretend you didn't hear it. You don't like either politician running, so you don't vote. When all the choices seem flawed, the voice of avoidance can speak loudly—telling you that you can stay quiet. And in cases where all the options seem equally bad, this may seem like the only sane choice to make.

"Bartleby, the Scrivener" is a lesser-known short story by Herman Melville, author of *Moby-Dick*. At first Bartleby produces a large volume of high-quality work, but one day, when asked to help proofread a document, Bartleby answers with what soon becomes his perpetual response to every request: "I would prefer not to." To the dismay of his boss, Bartleby begins to perform fewer and fewer tasks, and eventually none, instead spending long periods of time staring out one of the office's windows at a brick wall. The narrator makes several futile attempts to reason with Bartleby and to learn something about him, but eventually gives up. Bartleby is an admittedly humorous caricature of the conflict-avoidance strategy, but the story highlights just how sneakily effective the strategy is, especially against those who approach conflict through the voices of power and reason.

The voice of avoidance is a learned voice. It's difficult to imagine a two-year-old like Louie having his toy snatched away and then deciding that he just doesn't want to get into another fight about this right now.

What separates this voice from the voices of power and reason is its ability to hide—there are no outwardly expressed rules around avoidance or consequences for breaking those rules. There aren't any Fortune 500 companies that paint conflict avoidance on their walls as a core value or hold yearly conflict-avoidance conferences and workshops. And yet, according to Margaret Heffernan, author of *Willful Blindness*, when you ask employees, "Are there issues at work that people are afraid to raise?" over 85 percent of them will say yes.

The choice to avoid conflict doesn't come without consequences, even for the people doing the avoiding. Sweden's former policy of neutrality is a recent example of a country choosing to listen to its collective voice of avoidance. The country took this position due to setbacks in the Napoleonic Wars, in which it lost a third of its territory, including Finland, to Russia. The Swedes received a lot of criticism for their neutral stance in World War II, when they ended up supplying Nazi Germany with port access and some resources, and have since reversed a portion of their neutrality policy when they chose to become a NATO affiliate. Eventually, the voice of avoidance becomes as accountable as any of the others, but that accountability is a bit delayed. It's just a different way of optimizing for short-term results.

As seen in Sweden's history, a strategy of avoidance might work best when the conflicts are low stakes. When the world isn't literally at war and we aren't being held to completely unfair demands, choosing not to participate in a conflict has few negative consequences other than maybe annoying the more conflict-tolerant people around us. When we don't trust that anything we say will make a difference, it's easy to see why not saying anything is attractive—we get the same end result without the hand-wringing.

The only problem with this is that avoidance doesn't fix the problem; it just avoids the conflict altogether in the hope that it will go away, and so the problem hides for a while. The voice of avoidance is like the oxalis bulbs hiding deep in the soil, taking root, quietly biding their time. But while avoidance isn't the key to the art of productive disagreement, it does point us in the right direction: acknowledging that the voices of power and reason sometimes aren't enough. There must be a better way. And there is!

THE FOURTH VOICE

Our three default voices (of power, reason, and avoidance) were all inherited from our culture. They can all partially succeed at resolving conflicts in the moment. But as is true of yanking weeds out by the stem, their solutions are only temporary. Each voice creates shadowy side effects that stick around and eventually come back to reverse some or all of the progress initially made.

The voice of power creates resentment and polarization because it restricts options from being considered. The exiled options don't disappear permanently; they lurk out of site and will return perhaps even stronger when the opportunity presents itself.

The voice of reason takes shortcuts in the name of practicality and efficiency, and it tends to accept that high-cost, low-impact problems can be deprioritized. In the world of business, this flaw is easiest to represent as a cut line: everything above the line gets funded, with people and a budget, to be worked on, and everything below the line gets deferred to next quarter's planning process. On the individual level, it's encapsulated in the simple advice I hear all the time to focus on maximizing your strengths rather than working on your weaknesses. In a constrained and highly competitive environment, these are entirely reasonable plans! And yet that doesn't stop the low-priority problems and unaddressed weaknesses from piling up, merging, growing new limbs, and returning all the stronger.

Choosing to avoid the conflict by not participating doesn't address problems directly at all, even though it does buy a short-term respite from the anxiety of conflict.

These three strategies have driven human decision making for several millennia now, and the side effects and low-priority problems have had a long time to pile up and become even more difficult to address. In addition, our world seems to be getting into more and more trouble every day. The climate is changing, technology is fragmenting and selling our attention bit by bit, jobs are paying less even as mortgages, tuition, and health care costs climb and climb. Our physical and online spaces seem to be getting less polite, more anxious, and angrier by the day. On top of it all, we've lost the ability to enjoy a raucous debate about important issues with people who have different opinions, experiences, and value systems than our own.

There's a great migration happening as we abandon addressing conflict altogether. Many of us are actively considering, or have already begun, leaving communities and spaces and conversations that we once loved because they've become toxic and unpleasant. Some have even become dangerous. It's no coincidence that opportunities to colonize Mars are looking more desirable every day.

We're collectively anxious about our fates and our ability to cope with everyday realities. We are beginning to recognize our need for more time to work on ourselves, just to get back to the selves that we used to be. All of this ends up meaning that we aren't getting smarter, and we definitely aren't getting any closer to finding and building solutions to our problems. Why? We can't even talk about them. There just seems to be a lot more yelling—if not at each other, then into our pillows.

THE VOICE OF POSSIBILITY

"What are we missing?" "What else is possible?" "What else can we do with what we have?" "Who else can we bring into the conversation to give us a new perspective?"

The fourth voice, the voice of possibility, represents a way to approach conflict that diverges from the first three.

The way we argue is no longer working for us, and we need new conversational and mental habits to prepare us for today's conversational climate. The first three voices attempt to resolve conflict, because conflict is seen as a problem. The voice of possibility seeks to make conflict *productive,* in the same way that a skilled gardener realizes that weeds are merely unloved flowers, and sometimes those unloved flowers produce sweet, sweet berries that can make delicious pies.

Conflict, when we cultivate it, is like a blackberry bush that is accepted and integrated into the garden. It's watered, fed, and brought to health so it can play its part. In some yards, a blackberry bush is a reason to go nuclear, sacrificing every other plant in order to eradicate this pernicious pest. In other yards, it can be the centerpiece. There are ways to work *with* the blackberry bush rather

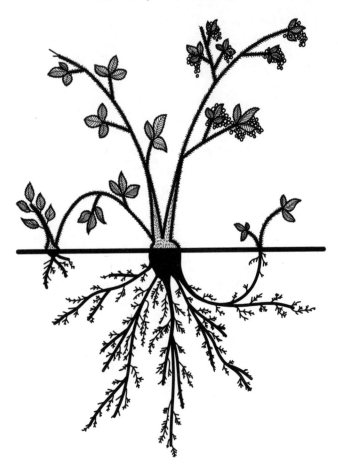

than against it, ways to turn the battle into a collaboration that benefits the plant, the garden, and the gardener. If that's happening, there's no reason to yank it out.

The voice of possibility encourages us very explicitly *not* to do what the other three voices have made habitual in us, which is to find a way to uproot and kill the conflict. It encourages us to step back from the automatic impulse toward resolution in order to look for *other ways* the conflict might be productive. It sees a disagreement as a sign pointing to something we don't yet fully understand, and seeks to learn from it instead of just getting rid of it. Our conflict-resolution habits, and our conversational habits that unfold from them, evolved out of an environment where taking risks was extremely discouraged in favor of short-term wins. The short-term win, the *resolution*, is what we are now beginning to question, because it's not the only fruit of disagreement that we're interested in harvesting.

In practice, the voice of possibility uses any spark of disagreement as a jumping-off point to find the source of dissonance. From there, it investigates other perspectives with deep curiosity until we're no longer surprised by the fact that the differences exist, even if the differences remain in conflict.

Instead of forcing people to leave your team if they disagree with you, show the work behind your decision-making process and invite others to find flaws in it or suggest improvements to it.

Instead of reasoning about the pros and cons of neglecting a hairy project even longer, open the door to suggestions about how we could make progress toward our shared goals within existing constraints.

Instead of dismissing complaints related to chronic frustrations that your partner seems to never stop talking about, dig deeper into the frustrations, looking for the real wish below the surface of their complaint.

Instead of breaking your back and cutting your arms wrestling with a blackberry bush in your yard, think about how you could turn blackberry bushes into blackberry pies.

In Stoic philosophy there's a common saying that encapsulates the voice of possibility: "The obstacle is the path."

Let's admit what conflict resolvers and conflict avoiders don't want to admit: we aren't going to be able to depolarize the political divides in our world with short-term wins. We aren't going to be able to solve climate change by squashing all debate about it and

forcing our solution through. We aren't going to be able to really dig into the issues of mental health, systemic abuse, corporate corruption, and extremist hate crimes with the solutions currently on the table. Our cultural obsession with short-term wins is part of the reason these problems are here in the first place.

It won't be easy to let go of our deep attachment to short-term wins. They're like candy for our habitual thinking processes. But little by little we can create room at the table for more possibilities, entertaining them without accepting them and giving them a chance to represent themselves honestly and authentically.

SECOND THING TO TRY

Talk to your internal voices

The voices of power, reason, avoidance, and possibility aren't the same in each of our heads. It's important that you take these skeletal descriptions and figure out how they actually sound to you. (Sometimes you can trace the voices back to people in your life; I often joke with friends that parenting is really just the process of installing internal voices in our children's heads so that they can hear us talking to them even when they grow up and move away.) The character of these voices determines whether we scold ourselves or feel compassion for ourselves when we make a mistake. They tell us whether our successes are deserved or not. And they guide us with urgent recommendations whenever we run into some cognitive dissonance and anxiety.

Who are these voices accountable to?

You! They're accountable to you.

What are they saying right now? Are they excited about this line of questioning, or are they telling you it's stupid? Either way, listen to whatever voice is in your head for a moment and try to determine if this is a voice of power, reason, avoidance, or possibility. Then ask it some questions:

What's urgent right now?

What's threatening right now?

What could I be doing right now instead of this?

How can I know if these answers are really serving my best interests?

What would happen if I did nothing?

The answers may come in the form of words or pictures or feelings or sounds. They might come through clearly or they might be really tough to pin down. This practice of "self-talk" isn't a sign of mental health problems, despite some associations you might have with the idea of "voices in your head." We all have these voices. Talking to ourselves is perfectly normal, and everyone does it without thinking twice about it. It's when we stop thinking the voices are coming from parts of ourselves and instead think they're coming from aliens, or the government, or some malevolent interdimensional beings out to destroy our reality, that it might be worth checking in with a mental health professional.

Assuming you're relatively confident that you can distinguish what's in your head from what's out in the world, talking to these internal voices can generate real insight. You may choose to have informal, free-form conversations with your voices as you drive to work, or maybe you'll choose to write to them and record their answers in a journal. For the purposes of this book, however, it'll be enough to simply give them names (power, reason, avoidance, and possibility work fine, or you can name them anything else that you prefer—maybe Paula, Rachel, Anna, and Piper?). From here on out, our only goal is to have some way to talk about them and listen to the kinds of things they typically say to us. What you talk to them about on your own time is between you and them. Have fun!

Develop Honest Bias

If we don't acknowledge our bias,
it will control us from the shadows.

f we lived in an imaginary world without bias, these three steps would always happen without a hitch:

LOOK   ORIENT   LEAP

Unfortunately, during each step of this cycle, we rely on special brain tricks, aka cognitive biases, to save time and energy figuring out what we're looking at, orienting ourselves around what it means to us, and then deciding what we should do. We might see something that isn't really there, or think it means something that it doesn't really mean, or take an action that isn't appropriate to the situation.

Disagreement between two people can be sparked by a difference in what you see, a difference in what you think it means, and a difference in what you think should be done, and those differences can be caused by these sneaky cognitive biases. It's crucially important that we get on the same page about what cognitive biases are, how they relate to productive disagreement, and what we should do about them.

Each stage of this cycle of observation and action ties to one of the realms of truth: the head, the heart, and the hands. For example, when we're looking at something, we're potentially dealing with direct evidence and are most likely to be thinking about "what is true": the head realm. When we're orienting that evidence within our own mental models, beliefs, and preferences, we're thinking about "what is meaningful": the heart realm. And when we've figured out what it all means and are ready to leap—to take action—we're thinking about "what is useful": the hands realm.

How does bias factor into all of this? In a big way, it turns out. No matter how hard we try, there are limitations to our own cognitive abilities that prevent us from being able to look, orient, or leap with perfect objectivity. Since research on cognitive biases started taking off in earnest, psychologists like Daniel Kahneman have discovered more than two hundred of them sitting between us and an objective perspective on the world.

SOME OF THE MOST FREQUENTLY CITED BIASES

Availability heuristic: When making decisions, we consider only the options that come to mind easily. Things that don't, for whatever reason, are therefore at a severe disadvantage.

- When we're thinking about a decision that someone else made, the options that seem obvious to us might not be obvious to them. Sometimes this leads us to believe that they intentionally avoided the obviously better option.
- When we are trying to predict the likelihood of something good or bad happening, we'll give more weight to the possibilities that come to mind easily—which generally gives preference to vivid, extreme possibilities that may be rare—than the bland or boring options that don't come to mind even if they are much more likely.

In-group favoritism: We tend to favor people in our group and give them the benefit of the doubt more than people outside our group.

- If someone is wearing a shirt that promotes the same college you went to, you're more likely to trust them than someone wearing a shirt promoting a different college.

- We tend to vote for, hire, and consider the ideas of people who are seen as belonging to the same demographic or community as us.

Loss aversion: We value things that we already have more than things we don't have yet and would give more to keep the things we have than we would have paid to acquire them in the first place.

- If someone hands you a box of cookies and then asks for it back, you'll be willing to pay more for it than if you were just looking at it on a table.
- We'll take more steps to avoid losing money than we'd be willing to take in order to make that same amount of money.

Biases alter our judgments and therefore create many opportunities for disagreement. Two broad, systemic simplifications of the world have an outsize role in sparking disagreements: we give the benefit of the doubt to people like us (which also makes us more skeptical of people different from us), and we assume that people like us are complicated and full of contradictions (and people not like us are simple and transparent in their motivations). From these two simplifications we generate a variety of stereotypes, prejudices, habits of discrimination, and xenophobic tendencies.

So can we blame biases for all the world's troubles? Unfortunately, it's not quite as simple as that. Most people would say the problem with biases is that we have them at all and the solution is to get rid of them. However, despite their reputation, cognitive biases are often useful. They aren't flaws in our thinking that we can simply repair; we can't run a debugger, identify the bug, give it a name, file a ticket, and systematically remove each one from our thinking patterns for good. Biases can't be avoided. In fact, the more we try to avoid them, the more blind we become to our own biases and the more distortion they can bring to our judgment.

Biases are here to stay because they're fundamental to how we think. Imagine how much harder it would be to follow a conversation if our brains didn't automatically boost the importance of information we've just heard (recency bias). Imagine how hard it would be to drive down a highway if our brains didn't automatically call out bizarre or different things to us even as we're having a conversation with someone about something completely unrelated. We'd be in big trouble without our biases, because we would be exposed to the raw fire-hose stream of information coming at us without any filters, without any means to create stories or decisions from it, and we would become paralyzed with information and options pertaining to almost every little decision we make. Biases evolved to soften the blow of information overload and uncertainty by creating well-worn paths of habitual thought that help us look, orient, and leap into action in a noisy, confusing, and often meaningless world.

The voice of power can tell our biases to shove it, but it won't work. The voice of reason can name every single one of our biases, in the hopes that they'll just decide to pack up and leave once they're exposed, but they won't. And the voice of avoidance can pretend that they don't exist, but they do. None of these strategies actually helps us deal with the very real presence of cognitive biases in our heads and in our communities. Again, we need to approach this in a new way!

The only way forward is to accept and eventually appreciate biases as a necessary and permanent part of what makes us human. The best thing we can do is to be honest about our own limited capacity to perceive the world around us. Recognizing this limitation opens us up to the possibility of relying on one another to help fill in the parts of the picture that we can't see and always being open to new perspectives that we might have missed.

THE COGNITIVE BIAS CHEAT SHEET

The idea for this book came from a project I started in 2016 to synthesize all of the two hundred plus known cognitive biases in the world, as described on the very disorganized "List of Cognitive Biases" page on Wikipedia. The post I wrote ended up reaching more than a million people in all kinds of fields, from psychology to economics to academia, and was also read by a lot of people who had more of a curiosity about the topic than an expertise in it.

In the post, I proposed the argument I just made: that all of our biases are there to solve problems for our brains and aren't really "bugs" in our thinking so much as shortcuts that are useful in many ways. Yes, they do produce side effects, but we can't remove the side effects without acknowledging that we have no other way around the problems that they solve for us.

I boiled down all of our biases to a few conundrums of the universe that limit our own intelligence and the intelligence of every other person, collective, organism, machine, alien, or imaginable god. All two hundred plus known biases are attempts to work around these conundrums. Out of sheer evolutionary necessity, we've developed skills, practices, and habits that help us compensate for these conundrums. The conundrums are:

1. **Too much information:** There's too much information in the world for anybody to process. Each of us occupies our unique position in space and time, and we're missing a whole lot of information about every other position in space and time relative to what we know about our own position. The only reason we can look at anything at all is because almost everything is filtered away first.

2. **Not enough meaning:** Nothing makes sense until we wrap it up in a story that we can relate to. Information comes at us disconnected and out of order, until we give it meaning by connecting the dots. This is how we orient ourselves to the world, but there's not much that prevents others from connecting the dots in a different way.

3. **Not enough time and resources:** We have to get things done despite the constraints we face in time, resources, attention, energy, and opportunity. None of us has the luxury of unlimited time and resources, which means we'll always need to leap into action with partial information.

These are big, gnarly conundrums of the universe that we don't have any chance of fully solving. What we can do, and what we have always done, is work within the constraints of these unsolvable problems. That's where biases come from. They make the best of what they've got to work with. Each of the three conundrums in turn has three to five broad categories of cognitive bias that function to help us work around them, ultimately adding up to the two hundred plus known biases.

How conundrums, strategies, and biases connect

Conundrum: There's not enough time and resources (hands realm)

Strategy: We stick with the plan

Bias: Loss aversion

Let's consider a common disagreement in the workplace: "Who should we hire for job X?" That might not sound like a disagreement in the traditional sense, but think about it. The whole ritual is an argument between candidate and interviewer. If the candidate can convince the interviewer that they are qualified for the job, they win. If the interviewer comes away unconvinced, they lose. And yet there's also a shared goal here, wherein both the interviewer and the candidate can come away being right, together, and use that outcome as a springboard to a working relationship that benefits them even more going forward. That said, even in this potentially high-functioning disagreement, there's a lot of room for bias to sneak in.

I was at Amazon in 1998, when it employed about two thousand people. Amazon, at that time, sold only books and CDs. It was in a period of hypergrowth that required lots of interviewing; by the time I left seven years later, the company employed more than fifteen thousand people. That seemed like a lot at the time, though last I checked (in 2019), it had more than six hundred thousand worldwide employees. It was the first job I'd had where I had to do a lot of interviewing. At first I hated interviewing because it was a huge distraction from the work I was actually hired to do. Part of my dislike of interviewing was also because it was super hard. It seemed so impossible to decide who should get a thumbs-up versus a thumbs-down based on so little time and so little information. I was also young and inexperienced and didn't really know what I was doing. How could I be trusted to evaluate someone else if I was faking it till I made it at my own job? Since leaving Amazon, I have been at Twitter, Slack, and several other start-ups during times of hypergrowth (it's a normal occurrence at many early-stage tech start-ups). I've probably interviewed more than a thousand people in the last twenty years, which isn't actually that rare in the tech world.

Consider this scenario: You're on the hiring panel for a candidate applying for a job on your team. The role is for a project manager—someone who has to be really organized and keep track of the many moving parts of a big interdependent project. They will need to have great communication skills, because they'll be talking to a lot of different teams, and these different teams won't necessarily report to the same departments that the project manager does. They'll need to be super detail-oriented, because it's their job to make sure nothing falls between the cracks. You're given one hour to interview this person and provide a thumbs-up or a thumbs-down recommendation for hiring them. This decision will impact the future productivity of your team, their careers, and a bunch of relationships within the team and in the broader company in ways that are impossible to predict. Go.

CONUNDRUM 1

Too Much Information

Information overload influences the head realm and looking.

Right out of the gate, we're not going to end up even considering a large percentage of qualified candidates, because there's no easy way to find them all. We put up the job posting in a few places where we think the right person is likely to see it, but we can't put it in every possible place. (And if we could, we wouldn't be able to read all of the applications.)

I've been a hiring manager for roles that received five hundred applications for a single opening. The first pass in these cases is often to distribute the load of applications among a few people who read through them and pull out the ones that stand out. What stands out is subject to our biases. We'll notice "interesting" things that confirm our assumptions about the right person for this role, and not all of them will be directly related to the applicant's competency.

Whenever there are more options than we are able to practically consider, we rely on these five strategies, representing fifty biases, to whittle them down to a pool of more manageable options.

STRATEGY 1: Depend on the context

We have a limited capacity to notice and remember things, so we use the current context to help inform what we should be paying attention to.

STRATEGY 2: Accept what comes to mind

Things that we've recently thought about or been exposed to are primed in our heads and easier to access than things we haven't thought about in a while.

STRATEGY 3: Amplify the bizarre

Our brains boost the importance of things that are unusual or surprising, because they are more likely to be important. The bizarre things could be threats or opportunities.

STRATEGY 4: Notice the new and different

When something new shows up or something changes, our brains call that out to us because it might be important. In addition to the change, we notice the direction of the change, which helps us figure out if it's good or bad.

STRATEGY 5: Seek takeaways

To reduce the amount of information we have to think about, we pay attention only to the parts that we think we'll need to remember later.

To develop an honest bias toward information overload, we need to accept that our selection process isn't giving every possibility a fair chance. We can then use this fact to spark conversations around selecting the best available tools and processes for whittling down the large number of options to create the best possible subset, knowing that whatever tools are used can always be improved further.

If we do this right, we won't become anxious when others point out that the process is unfair, because we already know this. Instead of reacting defensively, we can use their perspective to help us see how the process can be made *more fair,* knowing also that it will never be *completely* fair. Our conversations can focus on the trade-offs among various gray areas of imperfection, budget constraints, time constraints, etc.

CONUNDRUM 2

Not Enough Meaning

♥ Pattern matching influences the heart realm and orienting.

We use cognitive biases to turn scattered data points into stories that create meaning for us. The downside of this shortcut is that our search for meaning can sometimes conjure illusions: we fill in the gaps with assumptions, generalities, and stereotypes and then forget which parts we made up.

Most interviews I've done are either thirty minutes or an hour long. Sometimes there's a phone screening beforehand, and sometimes a follow-up round if new questions came up during the process. Afterward there's usually a discussion with everyone on the hiring panel about the candidate (either in writing or in person), and a decision is made. That's the typical amount of information used to make these large decisions, and despite its being not much, it often feels like *too* much in the roles where hiring consumes upward of 50 percent of the day. We have no choice but to construct stories that support "strong hire" and "no hire" decisions.

The most common way this construction happens is through pattern matching based on stereotypes around gender, ethnicity, religion, and age—all protected characteristics that you aren't legally permitted to discriminate based on. That doesn't mean it doesn't happen, because our associations with these characteristics are often unconscious in the first place. Given limited information, we have no way of evaluating an entire person and will use every proxy we can for signals that point to personality traits, competencies, and other soft skills that are evaluated during the interview process. We use these stereotypes to project thought patterns and future behavior on people. We also favor details that are familiar to us over details that are unfamiliar—our small talk is a subtle way of finding things we have in common with others, which will sway our general opinion of a person.

Take, for example, feedback like "The candidate wasn't able to give a convincing answer to the question I had about how they solved this problem" or "I didn't feel like they'd be able to rally a team of engineers behind them." There's no easy way to tie this feedback to unconscious biases, even when we're evaluating our own opinions! When I interviewed a few directors of hiring at places I've worked in the past, they unanimously acknowledged that this was a known and unfortunately unavoidable situation. You can try reminding interviewers to focus on evaluating specific qualities, but stereotypes are so deeply interwoven into our thought processes that being made aware of them doesn't make them go away. The only question we can ask is how we might reduce the damage caused by our automatic stereotyping, even if we can't eradicate it.

Whenever we have to come up with an opinion or story based on limited information, these five strategic shortcuts, representing 105 known cognitive biases, help us find the thread that makes the noisy world meaningful to us.

STRATEGY 6: Fill in gaps

We are strongly inclined to fill in gaps with generalities, stereotypes, and guesses to turn sparse data into meaningful stories. But after the fact, we often can't tell which parts were the dots and which parts we filled in.

STRATEGY 7: Favor the familiar

We imagine things and people we are familiar with or fond of as intrinsically better than things or people we aren't familiar with or fond of.

STRATEGY 8: Experience is reality

We generally assume that our experience is an objective view of reality and will project our current mood, mind-set, and assumptions onto everything else.

STRATEGY 9: Simplify mental math

We simplify probabilities and numbers to make them easier to think about.

STRATEGY 10: Be overconfident

We need to be confident in our ability to make an impact and to feel like what we do is important.

To develop honest bias about the way we build stories out of limited information, we first need to stop looking for interventions on an individual level. Making sure that candidates are evaluated by diverse hiring panels of people who each come to the table with *different* stereotypes does help point out and correct for some of the worst errors of judgment, but it doesn't completely free the process of stereotypes and generalities. It will always be necessary to remain open to new ways that we're blind to generalities and projection and to not become defensive when these are revealed to us.

CONUNDRUM 3

Not Enough Time and Resources

Constraints influence the hands realm and leaping.

We never have enough time, resources, or attention at our disposal to get everything done that needs to be, so we jump to conclusions based on what we have and move ahead. We use biases to turn stories into decisions in the moment. The downside of this habit is that quick decisions can be seriously flawed because they haven't been fully considered. Some of the quick reactions and decisions we jump to are unfair, self-serving, and counterproductive.

Being a "decision maker" is usually considered to be a valuable trait for leadership. At Amazon, a "bias for action" was even memorialized publicly as one of the company's fourteen principles of leadership. Amazon's website defines this principle:

Bias for Action

Speed matters in business. Many decisions and actions are reversible and do not need extensive study. We value calculated risk taking.

In Jeff Bezos's 2016 annual letter to shareholders, he expanded on this idea further by talking about the operational differences between Day 1 companies (his name for companies that are always operating with a beginner's mind-set, which is his preference) and Day 2 companies (the kind that think they've already figured everything out).

High-Velocity Decision Making

Day 2 companies make high-*quality* decisions, but they make high-quality decisions *slowly*. To keep the energy and dynamism of Day 1, you have to somehow make high-quality, *high-velocity* decisions. . . .

First, never use a one-size-fits-all decision-making process. Many decisions are reversible, two-way doors. Those decisions can use a light-weight process. . . .

Second, most decisions should probably be made with somewhere around 70% of the information you wish you had. If you wait for 90%, in most cases, you're probably being slow. . . . If you're good at course correcting, being wrong may be less costly than you think, whereas being slow is going to be expensive for sure.

Third, use the phrase "disagree and commit." This phrase will save a lot of time. If you have conviction on a particular direction even though there's no consensus, it's helpful to say, "Look, I know we disagree on this but will you gamble with me on it? Disagree and commit?" By the time you're at this point, no one can know the answer for sure, and you'll probably get a quick yes.

This isn't one way. If you're the boss, you should do this too. I disagree and commit all the time. . . .

Fourth, recognize true *misalignment* issues early and escalate them *immediately*. Sometimes teams have different objectives and fundamentally different views. They are not aligned. No amount of discussion, no number of meetings will resolve that deep misalignment. Without escalation, the default dispute resolution mechanism for this scenario is exhaustion. Whoever has more stamina carries the decision. . . .

"You've worn me down" is an awful decision-making process. It's slow and de-energizing. Go for quick escalation instead—it's better.

Jeff Bezos is famous for giving unconventional, controversial, and yet somehow extremely practical advice. He's particularly obsessed with constraints on time and resources as they relate to decision making. There's not enough time to consider all information and to convince everyone of every decision—don't even try. Disagree and commit. If it's a two-way door, commit to a decision, even if there's a 30 percent chance you're wrong and will have to turn around and come back. This has obvious implications for our hiring example. Some companies use a "hell yes or no" heuristic to encourage teams to give a thumbs-up to a candidate only if they're super confident that they'll be great at the job. That's important when a company is small and every hire has a material impact on the business as a whole. When you're Amazon and you're hiring tens of thousands of people every year (which works out to hundreds a day), the time constraint is real and should be considered.

Facebook's motto during its early days was "Move fast and break

things." Another common motto in Silicon Valley and other in-
dustries as well is "Fake it till you make it." Yet another is "Fail
fast." These sayings are all attempts at reinforcing a bias for action, because it's better than the alternative of hesitating and
thereby guaranteeing that a decision will be late without much
improving its chances of being right.

It's not just Amazon, Facebook, and our brains that have adopted
this attitude toward decision making. It's part of our culture and
part of our value system.

Whenever there's a cost to taking too long or an advantage to
moving fast, these final three strategies, representing thirty-four
known biases, help give us that necessary boost of confidence to
take action rather than delay.

> ### 🐢 STRATEGY 11: Stick with it
> We're motivated to complete things that we've already invested
> time and energy in rather than change course.
>
> ### 🐉 STRATEGY 12: Protect existing beliefs
> When our beliefs are challenged, we'll often automatically react by
> defending them rather than questioning them.
>
> ### 🐰 STRATEGY 13: Do the safe thing
> All things being equal, we'll generally take what we perceive to be
> the less risky path.

To develop honest bias when it comes to acknowledging our
need to act in uncertainty, we can take Jeff Bezos's advice and admit that there's a chance we'll need to turn around and head back
if we find out we were wrong. My favorite Amazon Leadership
Principle captures this well. Principle number four is:

Are Right, A Lot

Leaders are right a lot. They have strong judgment and good instincts. They seek diverse perspectives and work to disconfirm their beliefs.

At first this seems to contradict what we've been saying here so far. But if you read into the description, you can see that leaders are right a lot only *if* they seek diverse perspectives and work to disconfirm their beliefs. They're right a lot because they try to find out if they're wrong and then change their minds to be right. That, in a nutshell, is how we develop honest bias.

BUT REALLY, HOW CAN I BECOME UNBIASED?

I understand the desire behind this question. In the case of interviewing candidates for jobs, it makes sense to want to be less biased because you'll end up hiring better candidates.

White Fragility, a book by Robin DiAngelo that's about why it's so difficult for white people to talk about racism, provides an in-depth and masterfully articulated description of the paradox that lies at the heart of all bias:

> If we become adults who explicitly oppose racism, as do many, we often organize our identity around a denial of our racially based privileges that reinforce racist disadvantage for others.
>
> What is particularly problematic about this contradiction is that white people's moral objection to racism increases their resistance to acknowledging their complicity with it.

This theory illuminates an important point related to our goal to be less biased. DiAngelo is saying that when we see that racism is a very real problem in the world, we try to build an identity for ourselves that distances us from the problem. In racial terms, the phrase "I'm color-blind" has come to signify individuals who self-proclaim an absence of racist tendencies within them, because they perceive that to be the goal. Their intentions might be sincere—by distancing ourselves from racism, white people can more easily point to it and denounce it as problematic.

Unfortunately, it's not possible to be color-blind when the impacts of racism extend beyond our thoughts and into our institutions, platforms, and environment. Viewing ourselves as "self-aware" about our racial bias just incentivizes us to not look for it. The act of existing in a world designed to perpetuate racial prejudice means that, by being white in the first place, white people have already benefited from racism in innumerable ways: the schools they went to, the teachers they had, the jobs their parents held, the movies they watched, the books they read, the laws of government, etc. were all influenced by racism to uphold white supremacy.

I love DiAngelo's suggestions for those of us who want to be as helpful as possible within the world we live in, which involve internalizing some of these assumptions about ourselves and the world. Here's a partial list of assumptions she suggests to those who are trying to come to terms with racism in themselves and in society, which I've mapped to the head, the heart, and the hands:

What is true?

- Racism is a multilayered system embedded in our culture.
- All of us are socialized into the system of racism.

- Racism cannot be avoided.
- Given my socialization, it is much more likely that I am the one who doesn't understand the issue.

💜 What is meaningful?

- Racism is complex, and I don't have to understand every nuance of the feedback to validate that feedback.
- Authentic antiracism is rarely comfortable. Discomfort is key to my growth, and desirable.
- I bring my group's history with me; history matters.

✋ What is useful?

- Bias is implicit and unconscious; I don't expect to be aware of mine without a lot of ongoing effort.
- Feedback on racism is difficult to give; how I am given the feedback is not as relevant as the feedback itself.
- The antidote to guilt is action.
- Nothing exempts me from the forces of racism.
- Racism hurts (even kills) people of color 24-7. Interrupting it is more important than my feelings, ego, or self-image.

Her message is pretty clear. Should white people give up trying to be less racist? No. Will white people ever be exempt from the forces of racism? No. The big takeaway here, as it relates to racism and bias, is that *discomfort is key to our growth, and desirable.* Giving up—avoidance—is a way to resolve the discomfort and get back into a familiar zone. It doesn't lead to growth, and therefore it's undesirable.

Discomfort is key to our growth, and desirable.

Repeat after me: Discomfort is key to our growth, and desirable.

If you're a human being, this statement undoubtedly sparks some anxiety in you, and your voices of power, reason, and avoidance are jumping over each other right now with suggestions for how to respond to it. Listen to them without necessarily having to agree with them immediately.

How can we approach knowledge of our own permanently biased, racist, sexist, xenophobic, other-phobic natures that sprout from our location and orientation to the universe's three conundrums and not go crazy?

Hint: it's not by thinking we can rid ourselves of bias.

Discomfort is key to our growth, and desirable. Anxiety is key to our growth, and desirable. What is all of this discomfort and anxiety about, anyway? It's about wanting to have the answer, wanting to solve the problem. *Wanting it to go away.* To remove everything that's wrong and replace it with things that are right. To replace bad with good. To solve the mystery. To yang the yin. To escape the threat. To close the loop. To resolve the disagreement.

This desire to close the loop is embedded deep within our psychology. What happens when a sentence—

—hangs? Why are bread-sliced bagels so triggering for some? This dynamic between tension and release that makes us laugh at jokes, dance to music, and get out of bed every morning to see what the day has in store for us is the same mechanism that makes it really difficult for us to sit with something that's unresolved. It's incredibly uncomfortable.

The voice of reason tells us that we have to either find a solution or give up on the problem. Either way, it wants to be done feeling bad about it. In the case of approaching our own limitations in the universe, both biologically and socially, there is no final solution, but we can't ignore the problem. What we need to do is honestly acknowledge our discomfort and keep it alive in us, because it points us toward paths for growth. Even if there is no final, "all-grown-up" state for us to reach, we still need to take this path. We need to develop honest bias because it offers a place in between awareness and solution that allows us to keep the question open and to feel the discomfort of that open-endedness without losing the ability to function in the world.

THIRD THING TO TRY

Develop honest bias

If you take nothing else away from this chapter, take these four steps on the path toward developing honest bias.

> **STEP 1: Opt-in.** Developing honest bias requires us first and foremost to wake up to our own blindness and to stop trying to pretend it doesn't exist. Only you can decide if you're up for the challenge of taking it on.
>
> **STEP 2: Observe (beginner level).** Take steps to reduce the amount of time and energy you spend trying to hide or ignore your biases and blind spots. *For example, read up on information in this chapter to get familiar with the variety of biases. Notice when your defenses are triggered and check whether (a) you're really in danger right now, or (b) there's an opportunity to learn from a new perspective (even in a small way).*
>
> **STEP 3: Repair (intermediate level).** Take steps to reduce the time and energy it takes for you to identify and begin to repair inadvertent damage caused by your biases and blind spots. *For example, when you notice a blind spot, look into it and identify people and ideas that may have been under-*

valued or harmed by you and others. Look for ways to reverse that trend and repair damage.

STEP 4: Normalize (advanced level). Take steps to reduce the time and energy others have to spend challenging your blind spots and recruiting you to address the damage that you've contributed to. *For example, actively seek out information and perspectives that challenge your own. Invite the best representatives of positions you don't agree with to productive disagreements. Actively attempt to falsify your own beliefs.*

Steps 2 through 4 are essentially working toward the same goal of reducing harm caused by our biases, but the beginner level is reactive to incoming information and the intermediate and advanced levels become increasingly proactive about seeking it out. For step 1, which is all about accepting that bias exists and opting into addressing this fact, here's a contract with yourself for accepting your bias that you can adopt or modify to fit your own preferred aesthetic. It's a modified version of a contract in *White Fragility* that has been expanded to encompass all forms of bias. Mull over these statements and feel free to rephrase them in your own words.

I will try to accept my bias, which means I'm willing to:

1. Acknowledge my limitations and unique perspective.
2. Invite diverse perspectives to the table.
3. Listen generously when others point out my blind spots.
4. Be willing to accept the discomfort that this inevitably brings as a welcome gift.

In some ways that I can see, and other ways that I can't, I will always be forced to take some strategic shortcuts that systemically neglect certain kinds of information because of constraints of attention, meaning, time, resources, and memory. Nobody can escape bias, including me. Without these strategies, I would become paralyzed by uncertainty.

The strategies that I have to use also systemically neglect certain kinds of information that will disadvantage and harm certain people in a way that I will not be aware of without a lot of work.

Efforts to avoid bias are primarily about seeking comfort, which results in maintaining the status quo.

I must not confuse comfort for growth. Honest bias is rarely comfortable; discomfort is key to my growth, and desirable.

My biases are reinforced by my surroundings. This includes the communities around me, the products and services that I use in order to stay informed about the world, and even the institutions that I belong to.

There is no cure for bias, but it can be managed with honest self-reflection, requests for thoughtful feedback, and a willingness to address feedback directly however it comes to me.

Bias is deadly. We can't avoid it, and not addressing it isn't an option. This is an uncomfortable realization that I must nevertheless carry with me wherever I go.

I don't have permission to give up on trying to remove bias from my thoughts and actions. I can't allow myself to become paralyzed by the fact that I can never fully trust my own thought processes.

Paul Saffo, a forecasting expert and professor at Stanford University, wrote a popular essay titled "Strong Opinions Weakly Held." The title has become a bit of a mantra for many people in the tech sector because it offers a slightly unintuitive but practical way to keep one foot in action and one foot in acceptance of imperfect thinking.

Allow your intuition to guide you to a conclusion, no matter how imperfect—this is the "strong opinion" part. Then—and this is the "weakly held" part—prove yourself wrong. Engage in creative doubt. Look for information that doesn't fit, or indicators that are pointing in an entirely different direction. Eventually your intuition will kick in and a new hypothesis will emerge out of the rubble, ready to be ruthlessly torn apart once again. You will be surprised by how quickly the sequence of faulty forecasts will deliver you to a useful result.

It's not that different from Muhammad Ali's famous advice to "float like a butterfly, sting like a bee." Floating like a butterfly means we should be willing to change our minds easily and often, always looking for the positions that are a better fit for the situation. Stinging like a bee means that we still need to lean on those positions heavily and make decisions and take decisive action based on them.

We have to do this *and* invite feedback about our blind spots *and* be willing to see them without getting defensive *and* correct them in whatever way we can. This is not a cynical or futile or meaningless pursuit. Robin DiAngelo sums it up well:

It's a messy, lifelong process, but one that is necessary to align my professed values with my real actions. It is also deeply compelling and transformative.

Developing honest bias will eliminate an entire category of unproductive disagreement from our lives that comes about when we think what we're seeing is an unfiltered view of reality. When your beliefs are challenged by family members, spouses, coworkers, or friends, instead of leaping immediately to the conclusion that they're wrong, you can instead ask yourself if you might be missing something that they can see but you can't.

Instead of saying, "I know I'm right!" say, "I'm not seeing what you're seeing. Can you help me get there?" You don't have enough information yet to know if what you think they are saying is what they're actually saying. Instead of getting angry, get curious. Doing so will radically change your relationships to people, ideas, and the world by allowing new perspectives to reach you that would have otherwise been immediately dismissed. It will change which kinds of dissonance spark anxiety across the board and will create space for the voice of possibility to be heard more frequently and clearly.

Speak for Yourself

Our ability to speculate about other people,
their perspectives, and their reasoning is weak.
Instead, invite everyone to represent
themselves.

One of the most surprising things I've noticed during my
experiments in productive disagreement is how quickly
things go off the rails precisely when people stop speaking from their own perspective and try to speculate about other
people's perspectives. You may have heard in various conflict-
resolution best practices that we should use "I feel" statements instead of "You are" or, even worse, "You feel" statements. Of course,
it's one thing to nod your head to this and quite another to put it
into practice.

Our difficulty in predicting what other people think shows up
in many of the cognitive biases and strategic shortcuts we just re-
viewed. Two of the strategies in particular, number 6 ("Fill in
gaps") and number 8 ("Experience is reality"), help us first create
stories using stereotypes and generalizations and then project our
own internal states onto others as well as the world. We then
promptly forget which parts we got from the world and which
parts we patched together on our own.

We're just not that great at representing the perspectives of other
people when they differ from our own. We oversimplify them,
exaggerate their flaws, and fill in the blanks with stereotypes. The

antidote to these limitations is simple: our responsibility is to speak only for ourselves and to invite others to represent themselves.

WHAT CAN'T BE CONTESTED?

When we speak for ourselves from our own heart about our own perspective, preferences, values, and meaning, we reveal something that can't ever be contested by others. We are the primary source of truth for our own hearts. On the other hand, when we try to speak for others, we're speculating about things that we have no claim on, and those things can be contested entirely by others.

Therefore, when speaking of matters of the heart, we can easily get tangled up in disagreement when we speak for others or others speak for us. It happens a lot.

Let's use politics as an example, because it will show how easy it is to make this mistake and to get entangled in incredibly unproductive disagreements. One of the biggest, most unproductive, least enjoyable arguments in recent history came to a boil during the United States presidential election of 2016.

This book's journey, in fact, is a result of political conversations that sparked a lot of anxiety within me during the 2016 presidential election season. I was at my worst in some of these conversations, and so unproductive that I realized I had to find a different approach, which eventually led to identifying and refining my own art of productive disagreement. I also want to clarify that I of course have my own position and biases coming into broad topics like politics. I'll try to be as up front as possible about them.

I have a few friends whom I've been very close to since high school. We first met as awkward runners on the school's cross-country team, where we all self-identified as a group of freethinkers (probably more aspirational than actual). Three were religious, two were atheists. Two didn't even drink caffeine, a couple of others drank and did recreational drugs occasionally. A few of us wanted to get married and have lots of kids, while others wanted nothing to do with that stuff anytime soon. We all shared a set of core values as a group of friends who could respect differences in others, even though we were all extremely different from one another. As among many similar friend groups throughout history, there was of course plenty of taunting and poking and the occasional argument, but it was all in good faith. Good faith—a resource so scarce today—can be very plentiful in small peer groups.

Good faith—from the Latin *bona fides*—is a sincere intention to be fair, open, and honest regardless of the outcome of the interaction.

Twenty-five years passed. We all moved to different parts of the country and the world. One, Jared, became a lawyer for Exxon, living in Dubai, with five children. Another, Nathan, is a special-needs teacher in Texas, also with five kids. Chris is a warehouse manager in Florida, and Jimmy is a videographer and photographer for clients like Vice Media and Al Jazeera, as often in remote parts of Europe and Asia as in the States. As for me, I've stayed relatively put, working at tech companies and start-ups like Amazon, Twitter, Slack, and Patreon, as well as a few of my own, now rooted in the Bay Area with my wife and two kids. You can probably guess that some of us moved further left in our political leanings over time and some moved to the right. One friend, Chris, very stubbornly defended the very center, and we probably gave him the hardest time of all. Despite the friendly ribbing, we took pride in being able to discuss very different positions with one another in a way that everyone felt was productive and respectful.

A group conversation among the five of us about politics began in July of 2016 and continued all the way through the election. More than thirty thousand words were passed among us during that time, primarily back-and-forths about how we were each interpreting the same events from different political perspectives. November 8 arrived, and the results came in. Jimmy and I had voted for Clinton. Chris didn't vote. Nathan voted for a write-in candidate. Jared declined to share who he voted for. In the aftermath of the election, we were all in shock. Despite our varied positions, I think everyone expected Clinton to win.

I couldn't handle it. Something in my head broke. The conversation picked back up, analyzing what had happened from different perspectives, predicting the future, etc. But I simply posted, "I'm devastated. I'm ashamed to even be a US citizen. Hatred has won and our country is going to become worse for so many people. I'm gonna need some time." I had been recruited by the only voice that wasn't completely out of commission: the voice of avoidance. All I could do was walk away and pretend the conflict didn't exist. My friends, having different worldviews that weren't as conflicted as my own, tried to console me and give me some words of encouragement about how this would ultimately be good for our country. "It's a wake-up call," said Jared. "At least think about how this might result in some positives as well as negatives."

But I couldn't see it. "I can't. I need some time to process. I'm sorry. I'm gonna need some time." I was repeating the same words, knowing that I usually have more reasons to offer, but nothing was coming to me. I didn't know how much time I needed, but I effectively dropped out of the group conversation without a promise of returning. My go-to voice of reason had been silenced by getting so many things wrong. I had, in a single national moment that was the culmination of everything that had been building up over the past six months, simply lost faith in the idea of a productive, rational, honest conversation and so decided to avoid them entirely. (A couple of years later, looking back on our conversation thread, I can see my friends had made some solid points that I hadn't fully considered at the time.)

Meanwhile, the Trump presidency continued to unfold over the coming weeks, months, and years. I knew in the back of my mind that avoidance wouldn't ultimately be a very satisfying position to take, but I didn't see how reason would make any difference either. If I couldn't gain any traction with my closest, most trusted, deeply respected friends over the course of six months and thirty thousand words regarding a single decision about who to vote for, then how many words and how much reason would it take to reach the sixty-two million people who voted for Trump, or the almost one hundred million eligible voters who didn't vote at all?

The worst part wasn't that I couldn't figure out how to convince one hundred and sixty-two million people that I was right but that

I realized that I didn't know what I wanted to convince them of. I had missed something that had been very obvious to lots of other people. Unlike during other periods of severe collective cognitive dissonance, I no longer believed that we had the tools to find out if we were right. If it was impossible to change minds, what fixed them in place? Was it reason? It didn't really seem so, because if that were the case, then reason could move it. Brute force didn't make sense as a valid strategy for getting people to vote, and not voting or talking about politics at all would certainly only make the problem fester in its current state. I sincerely felt as though my country was a boat and it was sinking. Rather than doing anything to help, I was paralyzed—and also suddenly feeling implicated in the sinking. What had we done to cause this? What had *I* done? And what, if anything, could I do to help reverse it?

This is when the voice of possibility whispered its first coherent words to me. It was a quiet voice, asking me to withhold judgment for as long as I could, to allow contradictory perspectives to sit side by side without freaking out and flipping a table.

As this occurred to me, I remembered that Nathan, who was on the conservative end of the friend spectrum, had argued throughout the election season that neither Trump nor Clinton was worth voting for. He ultimately chose to vote for a write-in candidate, "We the People." He wasn't alone—the 2016 election saw write-in votes spike by as much as seven times relative to the prior presidential election in 2012. When I was listening to the voice of reason, this made absolutely no sense to me. In fact, I found it offensive. Our voting system was structured to encourage people to vote for the outcome they desired most. Voting for a write-in candidate felt the same as not voting at all, and not voting at all was the same as abandoning all hope of having an impact. All throughout the debate, up to the election, this option had seemed completely nonsensical to me.

Now, with plenty of distance from the actual election to buffer my immediate reaction of frustration, I heard Nathan's words differently. If, hypothetically speaking, none of the available options was good, could a vote be used in its negative sense by not voting? The voice of reason in my head had very reasonably pointed out

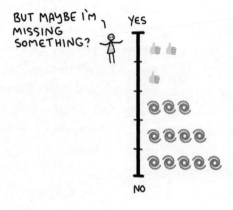

that this wasn't the best means to any desirable end. And yet, the way Nathan used his vote was his only tool to express his political stance in a system designed to give everyone one vote. If this was how he chose to use it, could I really make a claim that he was using it wrong? Could I tell him what his heart should feel?

The voice of possibility allowed me to recognize the possibility that not voting might be a valid means of representing oneself in a democracy if the goal is to give everyone a voice to speak for themselves. I say "might" because the voice of possibility considers it unnecessary to decide immediately whether an idea is absolutely correct.

In a very real way that I could feel in my own heart rate and blood pressure, the voice of possibility didn't lean on anxiety to increase my sense of urgency or recommend stomping out opposing opinions, but rather opened up swirling possibilities to explore and understand better on my own time.

EVERYONE GETS A VOTE

One of the side effects of listening to the voice of possibility is that open questions appear everywhere. On a normal day, listening to the voice of reason, I might ask questions like, "Do I want to open this can of worms right now?" and "What do I expect to get out of this conversation?" These were logical questions, and they made a lot of sense when I was driven primarily by goal-seeking and purpose-achieving activities. But now I had stopped having a destination in mind when it came to political conversations other than a curiosity to explore what I didn't know, going *toward* confusion rather than away from it. The way I describe this feeling is as a neutral mental space where contradictory ideas could mingle together, unresolved.

I decided I'd like to know more about what made this weird, seemingly antidemocratic action of not voting suddenly more popular. I realized I could research the nature of moral obligation. I could survey friends and family when serendipity opened up opportunities. I could reference other moral obligations I felt I had and see how they compared. I started asking people, "Do we have a moral obligation to vote?" in casual social gatherings and on my social media channels, and I got a good variety of responses.

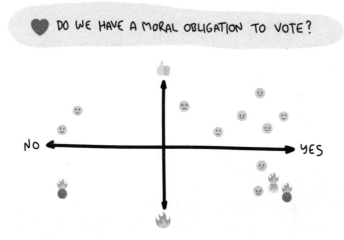

Some argued that we did have a moral obligation to vote:

I have a hard time with this. I see it as a responsibility. If you live in this country, there are so many privileges and benefits, some very hard won, and it seems to me, it's grossly negligent not to bother to participate in the system that affords you so much.

I see it as a common commitment to democracy. People who voted will feel they have a stake in the process even if it's small. More importantly, with high turnout, everyone will have a stronger sense that the result reflects the will of the people around them. The fewer people that vote, the easier it is to dismiss the results as unrepresentative and therefore illegitimate. An individual's vote actually shores up ★democracy per se★, regardless of their actual vote or its effect on the outcome of an election.

Some took a bit of a harder stance on it:

Not voting is selfish and negligent. One might feel justified in their selfishness because of various well-reasoned arguments, but it's still selfish. It's saying "my feelings on the system are more important than the real-world impact I could have in helping to support the vulnerable in my community through the tiny act of voting."

People who don't vote while enjoying the privileges our democratic system provides them are like players who don't attend practice or play in the game expecting a trophy when the team wins.

A few agreed with caveats:

I agree and think that choosing not to vote is a vote in itself. There are good reasons not to vote, if you don't understand the issues (uninformed), don't like the choices or if a person chooses to trust others to make the decision.

As the thread unfolded, the polite commentary drew to a close and the stronger-stance threads heated up. One person went with this rather provocative metaphor:

I liken the pressure to vote to the pressure to have sex. Many men believe sex is their wife's duty if they've been working hard to support them. It's not rape but it's not consent either. Can I just say no, or is coercion a de facto part of your rhetoric?

The pressure to act on the moral consensus is strong. In any case, this started a new side conversation, with a couple of people piling on the person with the rape metaphor:

> *I don't think I can have a serious dialogue with someone that likens voting to rape.*

> *Violent sexual acts are not analogous to voting. I don't even understand how that's not obvious.*

Notice how the voice of power is working to exile this direction of the conversation. And now that the temperature had gone up in the conversation, more entrenched positions were shared:

> *If you say my vote doesn't count or I'm not going to choose the lesser of two evils, then you're only looking at yourself. You're not looking at people in a weaker societal position than yourself (LGTBQ, POC, the poor, etc.). One reason I loathe so many libertarians is because they are in a position (often white, affluent) to be able to care for themselves to suit their needs. Their lack of voting is a slap in the face to those who need help. This country was founded and built on embracing the downtrodden—and if you're affluent and wanting to stay in your safe little enclave, then you're basically saying FU to those who are not as privileged by race and income. We don't just vote for ourselves, we vote for the community.*

This conversation wasn't particularly extraordinary, and is probably pretty mild compared to many other conversations happening in all corners of social media every day about any number of topics. It's useful, however, despite its ordinariness, because we can spot in it all of the concepts we've covered so far. There are many perspectives present, and many of them are in conflict with

one another. Each person is grappling with their cognitive dissonance, which sparks different levels of anxiety. And each person's
internal voices are suggesting different strategies to resolve the
disagreement, from confident reason to brute-force insults and
defenses from insults. Things got heated and then eventually died
back down, and I assume many people chose to abstain from the
conversation entirely because they didn't want to get involved in
the drama.

What could have made this conversation productive? How could
I have better routed the conversation toward productive disagreement instead of personal insults? Is there any way I could have
united the participants around a common desire to live in a healthy,
high-functioning society? What opportunities for growth, connection, and enjoyment do we have here?

If the voice of possibility doesn't provide answers, are these conversations a waste of time? If you are hoping to change people's
minds in this very moment, then it's easy to call this a failure. If
you are interested in having a productive disagreement that turns
this obstacle of a topic into a call for adventure, then it wasn't a
waste of time at all. It's a starting point, a trailhead. If we continue
the conversation, it might lead us to plenty of productive fruit. The
pursuit of resolution in a situation like this can often be wishful
thinking. We know our own minds are never changed in a single
conversation, so why should others people's minds be?

I ended up having a follow-up conversation with the person
who dropped the rape metaphor. I learned that she had religious
reasons for abstaining from voting: Jehovah's Witnesses see themselves as biblically obligated to remain completely politically neutral, which was something I didn't know. We talked about her
relationship to her church and the experiences she'd had of being
ridiculed by people outside the church, as well as her complicated
relationship with the church itself. This context helped me under-

stand where the strong reactions about consent were coming from, and ultimately led to an even better understanding of the complex positions that can be held on this topic.

In hindsight, I saw I had asked the wrong question. I had asked people to give me their opinion about what *others* should do, instead of asking people to tell me what *they themselves* felt compelled to do. When I reframed the conversation and invited people to share their own perspective, in their own words, it became much easier to see how each person could arrive at their own unique position.

FOURTH THING TO TRY

Speak for yourself

Speaking for yourself means avoiding two common bad habits: speaking for other people, and speculating about the perspectives of groups of people. It's harder to avoid these two habits than you might think. (See? I just spoke for you.)

For example, if I say, "If you don't vaccinate your kids, it means you prioritize your children over mine," I'm speculating about what your behavior reveals about your internal thoughts. It's possible that I'm speculating correctly, but you are a better authority on what your internal thoughts actually are. If I was trying to speak only for myself, I'd instead say, "I vaccinated my kids because I thought it was the best option for my children. What are your motivations for not vaccinating your children?" This leaves an invitation for you to reveal something about yourself that I'm not able to imagine on my own.

What if you're not right in front of me and I can't ask you this question? That's when we sometimes engage in the second bad

habit of speculating about the thoughts and motivations of groups of people. The opinion columns of large and small newspapers and online publications are filled with speculation about groups. Here are some excerpts:

> These anti-vaxxer parents—call them free-riders or even pro-plague—are putting my children and our communities at risk to cater to their erroneous belief that vaccinations would harm their children rather than contribute to the elimination of childhood diseases.
>
> —*Washington Post* opinion column, April 30, 2019

> I doubt that those who promote this line of thinking have really thought through the implications of what they are asking for: requiring *everyone* to alter their lives and actions in order to accommodate the most medically fragile, at all times and in all spaces. What they are demanding has implications far beyond vaccines.
>
> —*The Vaccine Reaction* opinion column, April 11, 2019

One problem with this kind of speculation on both sides is that it leans very heavily on our uncharitable generalizations about people we don't understand and then inflates them to the size of an entire community. We're bad at speculating about what a single other person is thinking, and we're *terrible* at speculating what an entire group of people is thinking. If I commit to speaking only for myself, my speculations must be replaced with the task of finding people who are willing to represent themselves as pro-vaccination or anti-vaccination. Then I can ask them how they think and act from their perspective.

Avoiding speculation about others is the difference between leaping to the overconfident conclusion that you know the intentions behind someone else's actions and first considering the possibility that you are missing something about how they are thinking.

If you speak only for yourself, you'll:

1. End up inviting people into conversations instead of just talking about them.

2. Improve your mental model for other people's positions much more quickly.
3. More accurately represent your own position to them, which means they will be less likely to misrepresent or speculate about yours.

Another side effect of speaking for yourself instead of for others is that you will be less likely to rely on group stereotypes in your arguments. If you're in an argument about whether or not migrants are misusing the asylum system to get into the country and you take this guideline seriously, you will need to find and invite migrants to the conversation to represent their own motives. Even then, they are representing their perspective and not the perspective of all migrants. Continue inviting people to the conversation until you have enough perspectives to talk about the issue without speculation. This adds a new dimension to the conversation and grounds it in reality. It will inevitably open up new questions as well, like:

- "Where can I find recent migrants to talk to?"
- "Am I referring to migrants from a specific country or am I assuming they're all the same?"
- "Even if they are from the same country, couldn't each individual have a unique reason for leaving?"
- "How much can I rely on one person to represent a larger group?"

The majority of disagreements that make use of group stereotypes and labels, attributing intentions, motivations, and behaviors that haven't been validated, end up being unproductive. If you follow some of the questions posed by the voice of possibility, the quality of the conversation blooms into something *much* more interesting. You might realize that the strategic shortcut of talking about a group in a generalized, faceless way was a symptom of an overly simplistic understanding of the problem. Once you understand this, the responsibility moves back to you to put in the work to build up that understanding to a level at which you can properly look at the problem. It may even reveal that you aren't invested enough in the real question to want to find a real answer. That's fine too. Either way, you haven't projected a false mind-set onto others and then attacked it.

Ask Questions That Invite Surprising Answers

Surprising answers carry the
most information.

Our biases are mental tools that help us converge on stories, decisions, and actions without becoming paralyzed by too many options or too much uncertainty. One of the best tools to balance impatience for a quick answer with the desire to actually land on the best possible answer is asking great questions. Great questions invite great answers, and the best answers surprise us by revealing something that we truly didn't understand before.

GHOSTS

Wouldn't it be great if we could just invite a ghost onto our favorite television talk show and have them answer a few questions for us about exactly what they are, why they're here, and what they had for lunch yesterday?

It would settle so many debates!

Are ghosts souls trapped on earth because of unresolved business? Why do they wear white sheets? Are they interdimensional beings that flicker briefly into our plane of existence, as surprised by us as we are by them? Are they figments of our imagination, projected onto the real world? Are they demons or angels or aliens?

Do you think ghosts are real? Where would you put yourself on this spectrum?

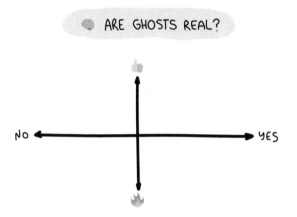

My position on ghosts has changed in the last year, partially as a result of experiments I ran while writing this book. I'll get into that in a little bit. But if you asked me a year ago if I believed in ghosts, I'd say that I didn't, not even a little bit. I've even had a few heated arguments in recent years with friends who can back this up. More specifically, I'd say that I strongly opposed the idea that ghosts exist but was open to new information about them. If a ghost appeared on my favorite talk show and answered a bunch of questions to my satisfaction, yes, I'd be swayed by that evidence.

If you go back further into my past, I haven't always been a non-believer. In fact, I once experienced a "being" during meditation that could be considered in the category of ghosts. At the time, I 100 percent believed I had seen a spirit of some kind. Now I'm pretty sure I didn't. Experience and memory are complicated, right?

When I was in second grade, a few of us neighborhood kids were playing with a Ouija board and it "instructed" us to search for something in the hills behind our houses. We found a buried box with some junk in it, and our minds were blown. In high school, I got into tarot and had a habit of hanging out late at night in diners and reading cards for other people in the restaurant. One time, a man I read some cards with burst into tears because he believed the cards had sent him a message from his recently deceased horse.

I was also very interested in near-death experiences and really wanted to communicate with angels and other beings on "the other side." One afternoon I was meditating and trying to invite an angel to a quick chat with me (as I had gotten into the habit of doing). When I opened my eyes, I saw an angel descend into my bedroom from the ceiling, glowing brightly like a reflection off a metallic surface. I asked it my prepared question: "Who am I?" It handed me a sheet of glowing paper. I looked at it, but it was blank. The angel promptly disappeared. My high school self, so desperate for answers, came so close to receiving them and yet ultimately got nothing—I was very disappointed! At the time, I interpreted this experience as direct contact between myself and a ghost, angel, alien, or some other multidimensional beings. Why would it go through the trouble of communicating with me and then say nothing? I *really* wanted the existence of such beings to be true, even as I was disappointed by them. Our minds are complicated like that.

Ghosts are complicated too. The idea of ghosts as the spirits of the deceased, trapped on earth, became the dominant ghost archetype during the fourteenth century, in Europe, but throughout history there have been many wildly different traditions and folktales about them. Spooks, phantoms, wraiths, specters, apparitions, and haunts have all made an appearance to people, all over the world and throughout time.

The idea of ghosts works well with the idea of souls and has been picked up by various religions going all the way back to

Egyptian times, and probably earlier. If they don't stay on earth, they travel to the netherworld, and often they require feeding and other offerings to ease their time there. Ghosts appear in Homer's *Odyssey* and *Iliad*; in the *Odyssey* they're described as "a vapor, gibbering and whining into the earth," generally minding their own business but sometimes offering prophecies or advice. Christians also have the Holy Ghost, which is the third part of the Holy Trinity alongside God and Jesus.

Prior to the scientific revolution, the idea of ghosts didn't necessarily contradict any other major belief system, but with the arrival of very powerful tools of measurement and a better understanding of matter and energy, that's not the case anymore. To date, no conclusive proof of ghosts has been found, despite the prevalence of sightings and ghost-hunter reality television shows. That brings us to the question: Given that there remain so many different perspectives on and interpretations of ghosts, is it possible to have a productive dialogue about them? If so, how? Let's examine it from the perspective of each voice—and while we do, try to notice which ones resonate with the voices in your own head.

The voice of power

If we're listening to the voice of power, we could try to demand that someone believe (or not believe) in ghosts, but generally the voice of power is pretty ineffective at making demands that involve belief. The best it can do is exile people who believe the wrong thing, or plug your ears and go "Blah blah blah!"

The voice of reason

It's very common for ghost skeptics to speak with the voice of reason to engage on this topic. If ghosts are real, why can't scientific tools detect them conclusively? If they're not real, why do so many people continue to report ghostly experiences, even among the scientifically literate crowd? Logic doesn't abide these contradictions and suffers cognitive dissonance when attempting to make sense of them.

There have been many attempts by various scientific communities to debunk the idea of ghosts. The physician John Ferriar wrote *An Essay Towards a Theory of Apparitions* in 1813, in which he argued that sightings of ghosts were the result of optical illusions. The Committee for Skeptical Inquiry (CSI), founded in 1976, puts ghosts squarely in the realm of meriting skepticism as well, and has gone after shows like *Ghost Hunters* by calling all of their conclusions "speculation and guesswork." For all their work, have they changed any ghost believers into ghost skeptics? That's tough to measure, but there's some evidence that the effort has only inspired believer organizations to dig in their heels and even attack. In 1977, an FBI raid revealed that the Church of Scientology had forged letters from members of CSI, claiming it to be a front for the CIA, and then sent them to the media to try to discredit the organization. The Parapsychological Association accused CSI of promoting an aggressive style of skepticism that could discourage scientific research into the paranormal, leading Carl Sagan to acknowledge the battle behind the rationality:

Have I ever heard a skeptic wax superior and contemptuous? Certainly. I've even sometimes heard, to my retrospective dismay, that unpleasant tone in my own voice. There are human imperfections on both sides of this issue. Even when it's applied sensitively, scientific skepticism may come across as arrogant, dogmatic, heartless, and dismissive of the feelings and deeply held beliefs of others. CSI is imperfect. In certain cases, criticism of CSI is to some degree justified. But from my point of view CSI serves an important social function—as a well-known organization to which media can apply when they wish to hear the other side of the story, especially when some amazing claim of pseudoscience is judged newsworthy.

The Independent Investigations Group (IIG) claims to be the largest paranormal investigation group in the world, and has a $100,000 challenge for anyone who is willing to demonstrate paranormal abilities or experiences under proper observational conditions in their lab in Los Angeles, California. Like CSI, the group uses scientific evidence to help increase skepticism of the paranormal, but by taking a collaborative rather than a confrontational approach, they're less likely to provoke attacks. On the other hand, finding participants willing to come onto their turf and put their beliefs to the test could also end up being a problem, and activity from the group seems to have died down after a few years of enthusiastic but fruitless investigation.

The voice of avoidance

We could of course choose to avoid the topic of ghosts altogether. After all, ghosts seem to also be entirely okay with remaining in the shadows, and belief in them doesn't seem to present a real threat to our day-to-day concerns. But while avoidance might reduce the chances of a pointless or unproductive conversation about ghosts, it effectively closes off an entire topic that might be productive to explore as well.

The voice of possibility

As of right now, I'm personally drawn to the idea of ghosts as unresolved open questions that have been given agency and a voice by our imagination—not unlike spirits of people with unresolved business, except mostly in our heads. Ghosts, according to this theory, represent big unresolved philosophical and rhetorical questions that defy satisfying resolutions. It's the act of holding open the question, "Do ghosts exist?" that creates a space of possibility for ghosts, and our brain represents that with a ghostlike placeholder (sometimes in visual form, other times in auditory form, other times just as an impression). Ghosts *are* unresolved open questions, living in limbo between reality and possibility. That notion would have a certain psychological elegance to it that satisfies my own wacky belief system—it partially explains why they show up in every culture (every culture has unresolved open questions), and also why they haven't appeared on any of my favorite talk shows (because that would resolve the question, which is entirely not the point).

That's a tour through my own current perspective on ghosts, which is different from my perspectives in past periods, when I held more black-and-white "They exist!" or "They don't exist!" stances. I got to my current belief about ghosts by asking a bunch of people about their ghost-related beliefs from the voice of possibility. I reassured them that I had no intention of changing their minds on the topic and just wanted to get a glimpse into their beliefs.

I asked people to respond to this statement:

Ghosts are a real thing that exists and can be experienced by us living humans.

To help me get a bit more information than a simple yay or nay, I asked respondents to choose a coordinate on this chart that best represented their position, and here's the distribution of answers from the group I surveyed.

Some overall conclusions from the results: 52 percent of people

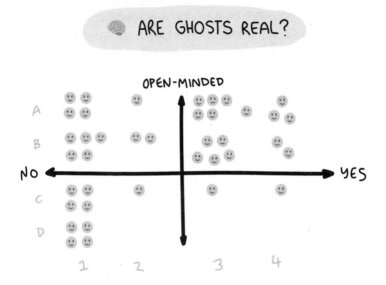

surveyed believed in ghosts on some level, and 48 percent of people didn't. Seventy-five percent of people overall were open to the idea of considering conflicting information, though this result was heavily weighted toward the ghost-believer camp. Sixty-five percent of people who didn't believe in ghosts were more closed-minded about seeing conflicting information.

Here are a few sample quotes from the nonbeliever camp:

I believe in electricity and that matter/energy is neither created nor destroyed so who knows what is left over. But I don't think it's a "ghost."

I have no reason to believe in ghosts but would love to encounter one.

Pretty sure that ghosts are not real and are figments of our imaginations longing for something beyond life. Talking about this with my wife to-

night led me to learn more interesting things about her beliefs (about ghosts AND aliens), so kudos for spurring conversation and learning.

And suddenly I realize that I am insane . . . C1 because clearly ghosts don't exist, and I would need very strong evidence to convince me they do. Except for that one time I saw one which puts me at B4 . . . and somehow both of these certainties exist in me simultaneously.

I am C1 with a caveat. I am terrified of supernatural things and can't watch scary movies or read ghost stories. So frankly I don't want to hear any evidence for the existence of ghosts because it would rock my belief system to its core, and that would make the world insanely terrifying to a point that would likely impact my mental state. Having a very strong scientific POV toward the supernatural makes life tolerable.

C1. I was raised in a hard-core D4 family—ghosts were fact. Many family members have personal experiences that reinforce their beliefs and I had to essentially "come out" to them (albeit very low stakes). So, it was a long journey to get to a 1, and it's still something I think about on a regular basis due to it being ingrained in me as a kid, which is why I'm not a D.

Pragmatism & logic get in the way of my mystic-leaning sensibilities.

I've seen some shit, man. But I still can't *quite* say I "believe."

And here's a sampling of responses from people who do believe in ghosts:

A3. Haven't seen one but know people who have. While I'm open-minded about their existence, it's impossible to prove something doesn't exist, and therefore my opinion probably won't change. But also have zero desire to argue about it.

I'm for sure a solid A3 most of the time. I wish science backed up my beliefs, but still refuse to give on my position given my personal experiences.

I am a strong C3 due to personal experience, but I'm not 100 percent sure that what we experience as ghosts are actually dead humans.

I've been in several homes that I couldn't wait to get out of. The engineer in me also realized it could be due to odorless chemicals in the air—I believe carbon monoxide poisoning can have that effect. I believe there may be a consistent form and description of ghosts across many different cultures and ages . . . and that's intriguing to me.

I can't imagine anyone convincing me that my own experience (not to mention the experiences of many cultures throughout history) is invalid, but life is full of surprises! I'm with others on here, that I wouldn't try to convince someone to endorse as well. I think this question involves a type of knowing that is outside of rationality.

I had my own experiences. I think so anyway.

I don't know how much we can totally experience as humans and I am not sure its what he means by ghosts but yeah totally.

I want to believe. And I think I've seen them before. But I have no proof, which keeps me from being a 4.

The stories that stand out to me are ones where people have moved among different beliefs over the course of their lives, and, as one put it, "Each transition point has a story in many cases."

The voice of reason would be interested in merging these accounts into a single narrative that worked across all of them. This is the never-ending agenda of the voice of reason, because in order to make sense of each thing it has to connect it back up to all the other things that roll up to the higher authority that gives power to the wielder of reason. The problem with this is that given a choice between accepting something that doesn't immediately make sense and discarding it, the voice of reason will usually err toward discarding. This creates a real cost over the long term, because new information and perspectives are ignored, often for way too long, even when they might have led to a stronger position.

The voice of possibility is less interested in integrating all of these accounts than it is in collecting as many conflicting perspectives as possible to put on the table and examine.

Some people talk about energy, others about gases. Some people focus on trusting personal experience even if it doesn't make sense; others focus on scientific replicability. Some are okay with internal contradictions, and others are much more adamant about having internally consistent beliefs. If we lay that all out, what kinds of questions emerge that we could ask?

A couple of questions came to me. Could our willingness to believe in ghosts be related to how much cognitive dissonance and anxiety nonscientific experiences cause us? Is it possible that people who get anxious about scientific inconsistencies tend to not believe in ghosts, relative to people who hear about someone's firsthand experiences and are more inclined to trust them at face value?

What if some of our beliefs are driven by our relationship to mystery versus science? I tested this notion with a second survey that asked these three questions:

Is astrology a useful tool for self-reflection and decision making?

    a.   Yes, the stars influence us in real ways.

    b.   Yes, but more as a way to spark interesting self-reflections.

    c.   No, but it can be fun to entertain these kinds of ideas.

    d.   No, and it does more harm than good to encourage this kind of superstition.

How strongly do you identify as a scientific and rational thinker? (1–5)

How strongly do you identify as a magical thinker? (1–5)

The results came back like this:

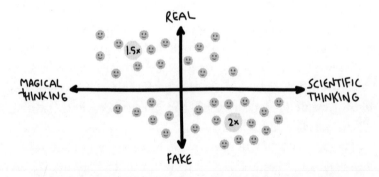

There's a slightly bigger camp of people who think astrology is harmful who also identify entirely with science and not at all with mystery. The biggest camp of people who believe astrology is real rated themselves as either equally appreciative of scientific and magical thinking or slightly more appreciative of magical thinking. Fascinating! I hadn't even considered this question when I started asking about ghosts, but now I was certainly surprised by this possible correlation between beliefs and preferences.

I reached out again to the people who believed in ghosts, but in one-on-one conversations rather than in a group, and began asking questions about mystery and the unknowable nature of reality.

One conversation I had was with a mother who was having trouble with her oldest son and had come to believe he was possessed by the ghost of her father, who had committed suicide just before her son was born. He was acting out in violent ways that she didn't understand, and in times of anger he spoke words about death and suicide that mirrored things her father had said. After trying many different kinds of therapy and treatment and counseling, she found someone through mutual friends who was willing to come to their house and exorcise the ghost from her son. The ritual involved setting up an altar in their house, placing herbs in various locations, and asking her son to recite words at certain times. After a couple of days, her son's behavior dramatically shifted, and he hadn't acted possessed since. When I followed up with more open-ended questions, the conversation shifted toward the mystery of knowing ourselves and the people we have the closest relationships with. The rituals this mother performed, whether powered by real magic or not, did bring her and her son closer together, which was the real goal.

The black-and-white question from the voice of reason that I *didn't* ask was: "Possession can't be real, can it?" I'm sure we disagree on the answer, but as I was slowly coming to understand, ghosts and spirits are more a language to talk about the unknown forces that influence us than a species of being that we'd invite on a talk show. If I could entertain the mother's mental model for a moment, I could ask much more interesting questions like "How has your relationship with your son grown?" and "How does your son make sense of all of this?"

I heard from another person—let's call her Z—whose friend claimed their house was haunted. The friend stayed with Z a few weeks as they sorted out a new living situation and believed that the ghost had followed them to her house. One time, a couple of things randomly caught fire in the kitchen. Z's hair changed color and became darker than it usually was. She found that everyone in the house was mysteriously quicker to anger. Eventually the friend found a new place and moved out, and the ghost left too. But other ghostly encounters kept happening to Z, to the point that she felt she was somehow attracting them to her. After things continued to get worse for some time, she sought out a therapist and through that relationship came to believe that in order to change these dark patterns, she should focus on health for a while. She moved to a new place, adopted a much healthier lifestyle, and a couple of years after all of this happened, she says she's a whole lot happier having worked through it all.

We know that our brains are story-making machines, and that we have a very useful (and weird) ability to turn almost anything into a face or a creature of some sort. When our brain sees too many faces and creatures, we call it apophenia, and when we don't see enough faces and creatures, we call it prosopagnosia. Most of us exist somewhere in the middle of the spectrum, which still sees faces in car headlights and the occasional ghost while also having the ability to relate warmly to our pets and to read comics. The voice of possibility acknowledges the desire to get to the bottom of reality but doesn't require it of us. I've found that asking questions beyond "Is it real or not?" will often reveal a much more rich and meaningful conversation on the other side. "What is your relationship to the unknown? What is it like to have sensitivity to nature and spirits? What becomes easier when you tap into your own health and relationship to the environment?"

Another person—let's call her S—recounted a story about how she had inherited a special sensitivity to ghosts from her mother's sister, who had died a little before she was born. Her mom said they had the same voice and handwriting. They both had eerie premonitions about things that were about to happen. Her mom's sister once said to her mom that their father was about to have a stroke, right before he did. When S was a child, one day her mother came to pick her up from school to take her to her grandmother's house. S calmly said, "Nanny just died." The drive to the house was forty-five minutes long, and when they got there, Nanny's caregiver informed them that she had just died an hour ago. There were many more stories like this. When we started talking about mystery and science and magic, S said, "I am willing to believe that it is just my brain, but how do we know that 'just our brain' is really just a brain?" Then a bit later, she said, "I believe in ghosts 100 percent. I am also 100 percent positive that the entire universe is way more than we could ever imagine and we really don't even know 1 percent of it all."

Each of these conversations ostensibly started because of a question about ghosts. In the past, I might have quickly agreed or disagreed with the story and then proceeded to reinforce or tear apart the details about what "actually" happened. But there's no rule saying that we *need* to do that—it's a conversational habit that the voice of reason has invented as a way to keep groups committed to a common cause. The "What is real?" question is the most black-and-white category and therefore becomes a go-to when we want to double down on certainty and confidence. Some of us have even grown to believe it's our *duty* to tell people they're wrong when they believe something our own identity group finds unacceptable. The internet gives us endless opportunities to fulfill this duty by presenting many more perspectives from a much broader cross section of the world.

"Belief alignment" is only one reason among many to have a conversation—and it's not even the most important one. Conversations are much more fulfilling when they function as a way to peek into each other's lives and talk about the real stuff we're going through: connecting with an unhappy son, taking on large lifestyle changes, or contemplating our relationship to mystery and the universe.

When the function of a conversation shifts from the single driven purpose of being right and discovering truth to a broader landscape of open questions and curiosities, the words and language that can be used to describe our experiences and relationships also become more rich. When I asked big open-ended questions, the answers were filled with information I never would have been able to seek out on my own. They gave me a look into the mental models and belief systems of people who see the world fundamentally differently from me, and I was able to acquire some of the language of their minds as well.

I no longer think of ghosts primarily as real-or-not-real, head-realm beings. Instead, I think of them as a heart-realm metaphor for the unknown and the unknowable. They give agency to mystery itself by allowing people to notice strange things they might've otherwise blocked out. In the head realm, ghosts aren't allowed to wander around and make weird things happen, because when it comes down to it, I still don't think they exist. My subconscious needs to talk to me in more sterile terms, perhaps using clinical words from biology and psychology books. But those people who have minds that allow ghostly placeholders for the unexplainable and that accept a broader spectrum of possibilities around every corner allow their subconscious to speak directly about what their experiences feel like, deeply, even if those experiences can't be scientifically explained.

Great questions create space for surprising answers to fill them. If we ask questions that can only yield answers that we already expect, we'll never be surprised and we'll never find a new wandering path through the world. But if we ask open-ended questions that have no predetermined answers, we can take steps farther and farther away from where we started. Curiosities can be piqued, and even better questions can be found.

> To ask a good question, walk right up to the perimeter of your current understanding about something and find a question that you don't know the answer to.

All of this questioning about ghosts led to another question I didn't have an immediate answer to: If we put aside our singular goal of resolution for a minute, what other fruit of disagreement will show up?

WHAT MAKES A GOOD QUESTION?

To explore the difference between a good question and a bad question, let's take a look at two games that you might have played as a kid: Battleship and Twenty Questions.

In Battleship, you've got some ships in an ocean represented by an eight-by-eight grid, and the other player has the same setup. Neither player can see where the other player's ships are, but you can "bomb" specific coordinates and through that process learn whether or not a ship is there. With each question, you can learn one and only one piece of information about the other player's ship, and through trial and error you can eventually sink some ships (hopefully before they sink yours).

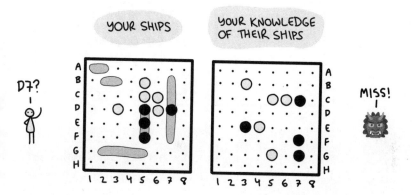

Twenty Questions, on the other hand, is a game in which one person thinks of something (which can be literally anything) and the other person has a chance to ask up to twenty yes-or-no questions in the hope of identifying what that person is thinking about. Because the game is so unbounded in terms of the thing you're trying to find, there's not enough time to ask super-specific questions as you would in Battleship. Instead you need to find questions that cleave through the unknown, without knowing exactly what will turn up. The perfect question in this game is one that divides the entire unknown universe in two and is able to know which side the answer you're looking for is on—as if, instead of asking for a specific coordinate, you could ask, "Is your battleship anywhere in A through D?" and zero in on it from there. If you're asking open questions like this, and the other person is still asking you about specific coordinates, you can see how you'd end up with quite the advantage.

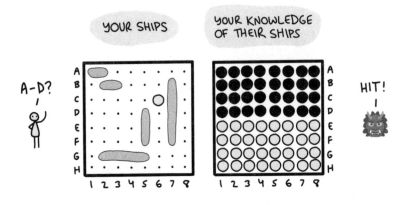

The questions we can ask in a disagreement are another leap beyond Twenty Questions because we aren't confined to asking for

yes-or-no answers. A good question can not only cleave the unknown into smaller and smaller slices but can also invite detailed images, stories, and dreams to be shared from the otherwise inaccessible corners of the other person's mind.

What does an answer to the question "Do you think ghosts are real?" reveal about the person answering it that can be used to ask a better follow-up question? What about the question "What experiences have led you to your current beliefs about ghosts?"

The first question is less likely to surprise you than the second, because even if you don't know the answer to a yes-or-no question, the spectrum of possible answers is very small, and you probably already have opinions about any answer that could be given. On the other hand, when a question is more open-ended, like the second one, the space of possibility is much larger, and there's a better chance that you'll be surprised by the answer. The other benefit is that the individuals answering will probably feel like they're being given a better opportunity to share their true thoughts.

The questions we ask help us build our own map of the other person's perspective . . . but the resolution, color, and sharpness of the picture is based on how well our questions draw out surprising information from the answerer. A bad question not only gets lower-resolution answers but also squanders an opportunity to create a space that the other person feels comfortable sharing into.

In real life, we're not trying to sink a person's battleship but to understand them. We're trying to create a map of a person's full set of beliefs, motivations, and knowledge. In real life, we can ask any question we want and aren't stuck with only yes-or-no questions. It's amazing to have a chance to peek into someone's belief systems and memories, a treasure trove wasted by a bad question.

There's just one final caveat that separates Twenty Questions and Battleship from our questions to one another. In real life, people don't have to answer, and if they do answer, they don't have to answer truthfully.

A good question requires, therefore, that the dialogue be reliably open and honest, and for there to exist some mutual understanding and trust that the information shared won't be weaponized. Without that trust, it doesn't matter how good the question is—the information you get back will be unreliable and potentially even malicious.

A good question needs to provoke an honest answer from the other player (meaning that there needs to be some agreement that this line of questioning is in good faith on both sides). Only then will it matter whether or not the question receives a surprising answer.

FOUR FRUITS OF DISAGREEMENT

Security, growth, connection, and enjoyment

If disagreement is a tree, anxiety and cognitive dissonance would be the water and air that help the tree grow, and the fruit that we have spoken of in passing up until now is what the tree produces.

A disagreement that's oriented entirely around the fruit of security will never yield productive questions, because in those conversations information and questions are used to attack and defend our positions. There's no reason to ask your enemy a real question, because the assumption is that they see uncertainty as a vulnerability and will try to use it against you—and vice versa.

In order to shift out of battle mode, we need to remember to value different kinds of outcomes, reorienting the purpose of the conversation away from security and toward growth, connection, and enjoyment. When you do this, incidentally, security also comes along indirectly.

Each of these four fruits of disagreement can be sought after individually, but the art of productive disagreement will ultimately show us how to seek all of them together.

Security

When you're being attacked, the fruit of security easily takes top priority. It's the original and primary fruit of disagreement, and the one we're still the most obsessed with.

Did someone try to take away your toy? Argue with them to get it back. In this way, disagreement protects your possessions.

Did someone insult you or your community? Argue with them to restore respect. In this way, disagreement protects your self-worth.

Disagreements themselves can be interpreted as a threat to individuals and groups. You're more secure in a group where people mostly agree with one another, and less secure in a group where everyone disagrees, because exile is one way to resolve disagreement. Groups, therefore, are incentivized to minimize disagreement.

Within the category of pursuing security are all of the things that the voices of power, reason, and avoidance generally encourage us to do: Resolve the disagreement. Get everyone to agree. Disagree and commit. Settle it and move on. Shut it down. Put differences aside. Agree to disagree. Put it to a vote. Seal the deal. Close the loop. It's the one-size-fits-all, habitual response to conflict and a big part of the reason why the way we argue has stopped being productive.

PROS OF SEEKING SECURITY:
- You gain immediate results of increased security.
- This strategy can be applied to any disagreement.
- By definition, it's the "safe" option.

CONS OF SEEKING SECURITY:
- Squashing disagreements will prevent other fruits from being found.
- Closing down disagreements prematurely in the name of security can give a false sense of alignment that eventually comes back in uglier ways.

Growth

The fruit of growth differs from the fruit of security because obtaining it often requires taking risks and sticking your neck out a bit. The fruit of growth is harvested at the frontier, while the fruit of security is most often found at home.

If you're in an argument about where to go for lunch, the safe bet is to go somewhere that you have been before and know you'll like. The growth bet is to try going somewhere new, in the hopes that it'll be even better than the places you've already been. There's a trade being made between security and progress, which means that this fruit is often found only after a certain minimum amount of security has already been established.

If you're alive in seventeenth-century Europe and are unhappy with your lot in life, the safe bet is to stick around and try to make the best of what you already have. The growth bet is to get on a ship and start a new life across the ocean. This is an easier bet to make if you have enough money to build a life across the ocean, *or* if things are just so dire where you are that they couldn't possibly be made worse by taking a giant risk.

You can see how seeking the fruit of security exclusively will lead you to a different argument than seeking the fruit of growth. If you're just trying to survive, you won't be as likely to take larger risks, even if those risks might pay off and give you more security in the end.

The actual manifestation of growth can be a lot of different things. It can come from a fight over territory and possessions, or a fight over a championship title, or a fight over which ad campaign will lead to the most new customers. Growth can be selfish ("THAT'S MY TRAIN!") or it can be collaborative ("Let's find out if that noise was a ghost or just a gust of wind").

PROS OF SEEKING GROWTH:
- The spectrum of possible outcomes is wide, which is another way of saying it's risky.
- By trading some security for the possibility of growth, you can potentially earn larger payoffs.
- Growth can compound over time, leading to more security than a straight bet on security alone would yield.

CONS OF SEEKING GROWTH:

- It requires an assessment of risks, which opens up the door for conflicts of head, heart, and hand.
- Risk can also lead to losses if you miscalculate, underperform, or are just unlucky.
- Growth can come in many forms, some easier to measure than others.

Connection

Sometimes the path toward personal growth is aligned with the path toward connection with others, but that's not always the case. Sometimes, in order to grow, we have to break off a relationship. And sometimes, in order to connect, we need to put our own needs aside for a while to better prioritize others' needs. And at the same time, if we seek the fruit of connection with others over growth, we may still end up with more collective growth over time. For example, when I prioritized understanding why others believed in ghosts over proving that my beliefs were correct, the increased trust and connection established opportunities for me to learn more about how different people think that would have otherwise been inaccessible to me.

Connection differs from security because it often requires putting trust (and risk) into other people's hands. For example, if I hear that someone has beliefs about guns or vaccinations different from mine, and I seek to connect with them around these beliefs even though I consider their beliefs unsafe in a fundamental way, it might lead me to see the world from a new perspective, or to consider a new edge case, outcomes that ultimately benefit me more than seeking only to protect myself from the threat of their beliefs.

As with the fruit of growth, the fruit of connection also benefits from a foundation of safety relative to the threat. I'm more willing to let a stranger into my house to hear about their candidate's positions if I don't consider them a threat to my direct safety. And on the flip side, building connections with people successfully will improve our security.

PROS OF SEEKING CONNECTION:
- Building connections with others also leads to growth and security over time.
- We're social creatures who find enormous fulfillment in relationships and are much less anxious and more resilient when we have strong relationships surrounding us.

CONS OF SEEKING CONNECTION:
- Trust takes a long time to build. As they say, it's earned in drops and lost in buckets.
- Trust can be betrayed in costly ways.

Enjoyment

Enjoyment is a fruit that binds many of the other fruits together but can also play against them. Enjoyment differs from connection when it comes at others' expense. For example, making fun of someone can both bind your immediate group together and push others away. How many insults and examples of systemic harassment and abuse are framed as jokes, but are anything but enjoyable to those who are the butt of them?

There is a way to enjoy a disagreement without sacrificing connection and growth. There's a certain kind of friendship—perhaps you can think of examples from your own life—where a long-lasting, innocuous disagreement even helps hold the friendship together. I love arguing about whether or not artificial intelligence is an existential risk to humanity with my friend Rick. I love arguing about whether or not the ends justify the means with my friend Tony. I love arguing about whether colleges will remain relevant in twenty years with my friend Carinna. Not all friendships have core disagreements, but there's no doubt that they can add something enjoyable to the relationships that do have them.

PROS OF SEEKING ENJOYMENT:
- Seeking enjoyment helps motivate us on long journeys of growth and connection.
- The spark of enjoyment is a clear antidote to the spark of anxiety.
- Following our enjoyment is a way of understanding our inner interests better.

CONS OF SEEKING ENJOYMENT:
- Sometimes enjoyment can come at a cost, if it's used to belittle.
- [Insert all cautionary tales of chronic hedonism here.]

An abundance of fruit

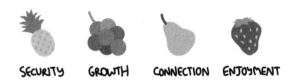

SECURITY   GROWTH   CONNECTION   ENJOYMENT

If your only goal in a disagreement is to increase security, either by battling threats or by minimizing conflict within a certain environment, you will never ask wide-open questions that enlist everyone in a collaboration toward growth, connection, and enjoyment. It's just not how that mind-set works. The voices of power, reason, and avoidance don't really want the vulnerability that a big open question creates, because that would give power to the other side.

At the same time, the other three fruits of disagreement aren't as valuable as the fruit of security on their own. What good is learning something new if it's then taken away from you? What good is building relationships with others if they use them to betray you? What good is enjoying a conversation if you're also being robbed at the same time? Short answer: it isn't any good.

In the long term, though, the fruits of growth, connection, and enjoyment outweigh the immediate and obvious value of security. Ultimately, productive disagreements return the same or more security *in addition* to the other three fruits.

Accepting this truth is the mental shift we need to make.

The battle for security is a zero-sum game. Because it assumes bad faith, it creates an eat-or-be-eaten environment for disagreement. If I'm safe, it means that the other side is weaker than my side, and the incentive for me in disagreements is to maintain that position of superiority. Security is a scarce fruit acquired in win-lose situations.

The battle for security, growth, connection, and enjoyment *together*, on the other hand, create a non-zero-sum game. To be "non-zero-sum" means that it's possible for both sides to win, and it may even be the case that helping the other side grow, seeking to connect with them in meaningful ways, and finding ways to enjoy the thrill of productive disagreement together are strategies that beat a battle for security alone. Is it possible that by seeking all of the fruits together, you might expose vulnerabilities in yourself that the other side then uses against you? Yes. But that's only more reason to listen to the voice of possibility about how connection can be improved, and how you can grow together and shift the environment away from one where the dynamic is about attacking and defending vulnerabilities in the first place.

FIFTH THING TO TRY

Ask questions that invite surprising answers

If you're stuck in an argument with someone and are frustrated and confused and have no idea how any of this will ever get resolved, it's possible that what you need is a better question. Here are a few questions that you can bring to almost any disagreement:

What formative events in your life brought you to this belief?

What's really at stake here?

What's complicated about your position here that people don't usually notice at first?

If what you believe was proven conclusively true to its staunchest opponents, what would happen?

What would have to be true for you to change your mind about this?

What other possibilities might we be missing that would change how we each thought about this?

Imagine a world where this is no longer a problem. How did we get there?

The bigger the question and the more surprising the potential answers can be, the better.

Generous listening

Of course, it should probably be obvious that if you ask a good question, you also have to listen to the answer. It helps, in fact, if the answers are surprising. Surprising answers trigger strategy number 3 (amplify the bizarre) to get past our usual filters, but it's not always enough.

Krista Tippett, author of *Becoming Wise* and host of *On Being*, a radio show and podcast that excels at asking productive questions, has this to say about generous listening:

> Listening is more than being quiet while the other person speaks until you can say what you have to say. . . . Generous listening is powered by curiosity, a virtue we can invite and nurture in ourselves to render it instinctive. It involves a kind of vulnerability—a willingness to be surprised, to let go of assumptions and take in ambiguity. The listener wants to understand the humanity behind the words of the other, and patiently summons one's own best self and one's own best words and questions. . . . In American life, we trade mostly in answers—competing answers—and in questions that corner, incite, or entertain. In journalism we have a love affair with the "tough" question, which is often an assumption masked as an inquiry and looking for a fight. . . . My only measure of the strength of a question now is in the honesty and eloquence it elicits.

As you practice generous listening, you'll notice a feedback loop kicks in and motivates you to continue down a path of great questions leading to surprising answers. Asking questions whose answers could surprise you creates space for honesty and eloquence. Honesty and eloquence increase the reward of generous listening, which helps you update your mental map of a person's inner world to be more accurate, which then leads to even better questions and understanding in the next round.

In Twenty Questions, the goal is to narrow down the universe to a single answer. Here the goal is to paint the biggest, most interesting and fruitful picture you can of someone else's perspective.

Build Arguments Together

Nutpicking and straw men produce no fruit.

f your motivation is to win an argument and claim the fruit of security, the best strategy is to pick the weakest opponents from the crowd, like a lion hunting for food. My favorite term for this bad habit is *nutpicking*—we pick out the nuttiest nut we can find on the opposing side, because they're the easiest to tear apart. They can then do the same for our side, and the cycle never ends. Nuts galore! When we resort to nutpicking, it's a sign that we're heading into an unproductive disagreement, even if in the moment it feels like we "won." There's no reason to ask a nut a question that you don't know the answer to—not only do you not trust their information, but asking an open-ended question gives them insight into your own vulnerabilities that could potentially be used against you. It's bad-faith dialogue all around.

If your motivation is to harvest as much security, growth, connection, *and* enjoyment as possible from a disagreement, and you have identified a frontier of possibilities that you think someone can help you explore with surprising answers to your questions, then you're not going to search for the weakest representatives of the other perspective to question. You're going to look for the wisest and healthiest members, because they will have the best information and hopefully the most surprising answers to your questions.

In fact, if you want to harvest all four fruits, it even makes sense to help the opposition build the strongest possible argument for their side, and to enlist them in helping you build up your argument as well. Only then is it possible for the outcome of the argument to be greater than the cost of having it.

Remember cognitive strategy number 7: Favor the familiar? This strategy creates a blind spot when it comes to building our own arguments, because we end up being a bit too lenient on ourselves. But it actually makes us great at identifying flaws in other people's arguments. Which means the reverse is also true—our opponents are better equipped to identify the flaws in our arguments than we are. You can use this quirk of the mind to make your argument stronger!

THE MONKEY'S PAW

In the fantastic short story "The Monkey's Paw" by W. W. Jacobs, a family is visited by an old friend one night who tells them about a magical monkey's paw in his possession that had a spell put on it to grant the owner three wishes. The only caveat is that the wishes are fulfilled in a way that generally causes the person to regret their wish.

The husband and wife in the story find this intriguing and immediately begin daydreaming about having more hands so they could get more done around the house. The old friend is horrified by this suggestion, presumably still grieving whatever bad side effects have come his way via his own three wishes, and he tells them to be more careful about what they wish for. He throws the monkey's paw into the fire, saying that it's for the best to destroy it. But the husband retrieves it and says he wants to give it a try.

The friend listens to his voice of avoidance and lets the family keep the monkey's paw rather than continuing the discussion or helping them avoid his own mistakes.

Once the friend leaves, the son suggests that they wish for enough money to pay off their house. It seems harmless enough, not even very greedy, and the father makes the wish. The next day, the couple receive the news that their son was killed at the factory where he worked, and the factory owners would like to express their sorrow by giving the couple a small amount of money, which incidentally is exactly how much they had wished for. Oops.

The story continues in this grim manner, eventually making its point that we're unable to see the loopholes in our own desires. However, the story doesn't really satisfy my curiosity about what would have happened if the friend had stayed around to help them phrase their wishes to be as loophole free as possible and hadn't just shrugged and left.

The disillusioned friend was the perfect person to poke holes in the family's wishes, because he didn't have the same blind spots that they did.

This principle applies to our arguments as well. The people who oppose your perspective are the best people to point to your blind spots and help you avoid making mistakes or fighting for the wrong thing.

GUNS

There are a lot of strong opinions in the United States right now about gun control, gun rights, and the curbing of gun deaths in a country that also believes strongly in the Second Amendment right to bear arms. There are also a lot of ideas about what to do. There isn't much productive disagreement coming out of this conversation, either in private circles or in the public political arena. How might the voice of possibility enter this conversation?

Let's pretend that you have a brother who is very pro gun control and an aunt who is very pro gun rights. You witness them diving into a flame war on your aunt's Facebook page about the latest mass shooting, going back and forth about whether or not gun control in our country needs to be more strict. This is a big, heated topic to unpack. Guns, gun control, and gun violence, especially within the United States, have instigated countless personal and national debates. Guns are also a literal symbol of conflict—the last resort when stakes are high and reason has failed us.

Though this is currently a very American debate—other countries don't have the same insistence on a right to bear arms—the question at the heart of it is universal: what are my rights to protect myself and live in a nonhostile environment? It just so happens that there are different perspectives on whether or not that protection and nonhostile environment come from owning a gun or from living in a place where people don't own guns.

So what can we do? Let's consider what we've already learned.

We can watch where anxiety sparks in our own heads and listen to our inner voices about what they think should be done. Is it the voice of power, reason, avoidance, or possibility that takes the stage? Can we acknowledge our bias and blind spots honestly even before we dive into the debate? What big open-ended questions can we ask that would potentially lead to surprising answers? Once we've done all of that, we'll see the benefits of building arguments together, with the smartest people and ideas collected from all parties.

What sparks anxiety when we talk about guns?

Take these statements in and pay attention to the internal conflicts that spark anxiety, generating immediate responses from your inner voices. Notice the intensity of each spark—some will be small, barely noticeable, while others could crash onto the scene like the Kool-Aid Man.

RATE YOUR ANXIETY

Stricter gun-control laws will reduce gun violence and gun deaths. It's simple math.

Gun-control laws infringe on the right to self-defense and deny people a sense of safety.

Guns don't kill people, people do.

The only thing that stops a bad guy with a gun is a good guy with a gun.

Guns are rarely used in self-defense and don't actually make people safer.

The Second Amendment doesn't guarantee an unlimited right to own guns; it was meant to help states maintain a militia, not to enable anybody that wanted a gun.

The Second Amendment protects individual gun ownership and is a founding principle of our country.

Most likely, at least a couple of these lines sparked some anxiety within you. Were the sparks 1s, 5s, or somewhere in between? If you imagine talking to someone who said something like this to you, you can probably walk, step-by-step, through a slow-motion conflict reenactment and tease apart the perspectives that sparked the anxiety, name the voice that spoke up in response, and examine the recommendation for the right course of action. Do you naturally gravitate toward fighting back with power and reason, shrink away and avoid disagreement entirely, or approach the conflict with open-ended questions?

What is the end game for the gun-control debate?

In their Facebook flame war, your brother and aunt each see the other as a threat to their worldview, way of life, and even home. Your brother believes that schools and other public venues are becoming less safe because it takes only one unhappy person with a semiautomatic rifle to kill dozens of innocent people. He feels America's standing in the world is dropping because we can't even protect our own citizens against one another, and he's blaming people like your aunt for allowing this to happen. On the other hand, your aunt believes that America was founded on a belief in the importance of self-reliance and personal freedom. She feels America's standing in the world is dropping because we can't trust citizens to be free, and she blames people like your brother for trying to take this freedom away from others.

Despite their differences in worldview and opinions about the greatest threats the country faces, your brother and aunt both live in the same country. They both believe that their country and the American dream are threatened by the politics of the other. Stakes are high. Kids are dying in schools. The Constitution is under threat. And since there's only one America to split among us all, a mutual victory seems hard to imagine.

Head realm: what is true?

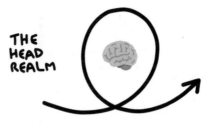

What disagreements about information might we be able to notice and call out from this conversation? First, how little each side understands the other—information is not flowing well between them. A 2017 study revealed that members of different political parties were much worse at guessing qualities of the other party than they were of their own. For example, Republicans, on average, estimated that 46 percent of Democrats were African American, but the real number is closer to 25 percent. On the other hand, Democrats, on average, estimated that 44 percent of Republicans were over the age of sixty-five, when in fact the real number is only 21 percent. People weren't great at guessing their own party's numbers either, but they weren't nearly as bad as they were at guessing the other party's.

How informed are we even about our own position on guns? We're definitely all up-to-date on the big headlines that have been broadcast on the news and in the press, but I was surprised to realize just how little I knew about gun-control legislation in California, where I live. Once I realized this, it was easy to learn that California has some of the strictest gun-control laws in our country. When I conducted a survey amongst a hundred or so friends and asked them what laws they thought California should change, most of them proposed laws that are already on the books. California requires background checks on all gun sales, for example, even at gun shows. California also requires firearm safety training and certification in order to own a gun.

Every fiber of our brains is wired to be overconfident in our own side's arguments and to be overly skeptical of the other side's (strategy number 7: Favor the familiar; strategy number 9: Be overconfident). This leaves us extremely ill prepared to take a disagreement off the beaten path of well-rehearsed headlines and shocking facts, because we don't really have any tools to rely on in those conversations.

Heart realm: what is meaningful?

One example of different preferences and values leading to disagreement can be seen in how people interpret the Second Amendment, and various facts about gun ownership and gun homicides, depending on their own value system.

The Second Amendment to the United States Constitution states: "A well regulated Militia, being necessary to the security of a free State, the right of the people to keep and bear Arms, shall not be infringed." Everyone acknowledges the Second Amendment is law, of course, so the information itself is not up for debate. However, your brother claims the most important part of the sentence is "a well regulated Militia," meaning that this doesn't apply to individuals. Your aunt, on the other hand, focuses on "the right of the people to keep and bear Arms, shall not be infringed" as the most important part. One true statement, two interpretations that can be used as weapons against the other side in a bad-faith conflict.

According to the Pew Research Center, in 2013: "There are by various estimates anywhere from 270 million to 310 million guns in the United States—close to one firearm for every man, woman and child. But only a minority of Americans own guns." From another Pew Research Center study a few years later, they added: "Today, three-in-ten U.S. adults say they own a gun, and an additional 36 percent say that while they don't own one now, they might be open to owning a gun in the future. A third of adults say they don't currently own a gun and can't see themselves ever doing so." Your brother talks about the number of guns in the country, comparing it to the population of the country as a way to imply that it's ridiculously high. Your aunt, on the other hand, uses the three-out-of-ten number to highlight both how unreliable the gun count is, but to also downplay the number of gun owners in the country. Same information, different interpretation and values placed on that information.

According to the Centers for Disease Control and Prevention, which tracks mortality rates across the country every year: "In 2015, 36,252 persons died from injury by firearms in the United States." The death rate for injury by firearms was 11 out of 100,000 people. This is about 17 percent of all injury-related deaths, which includes car accidents, drug overdoses, and many other things but doesn't include illness and health-related deaths. If you count all illness-related deaths as well, firearms accounted for 0.09 percent of all 39.5 million deaths in 2015. Your brother focuses primarily on the 36,252 deaths and compares this number to statistics in other countries to point out how big of a problem death by firearm injury is. Your aunt focuses on the fact that this is a tiny fraction of the number of deaths happening every year. She asks why we should focus on this number so much and not on the fact that the numbers of people dying from car accidents and even from falling are comparable. She uses this information to cast your brother's intentions as being clearly motivated by a cultural agenda and not just a public safety one.

You can see how your brother and your aunt, when listening to the voices of reason and power, use information as a weapon intended to harm the other side, even if it requires interpreting information to suit their purpose. From the outside, it seems like this disagreement can possibly be resolved with information, but it's really the values underneath the information that are powering the disagreement. A conflict of heart can't be solved with facts and figures; it needs to be addressed in other much slower and more subtle ways.

You can see this reality clearly when leaders who enter this debate don't come forward with information but instead appeal to emotions and a sense of what is sacred to their communities. Charlton Heston, for example, who was president of the National Rifle Association (NRA) for many years, said in a famous 2000 political speech: "As we set out to defeat the divisive forces that would take freedom away, I want to say these fighting words for everyone within the sound of my voice to hear and to heed: I'll give you my gun when you pry it from my cold, dead hands!" This was obviously not intended to be an invitation to a conversation about guns but rather a shot fired across the bow of the Democratic Party that mostly functioned to reinforce the gun-owning community's core values of freedom and independence.

Barack Obama, during his 2008 presidential campaign, spoke at a fundraiser in California and said: "You go into some of these small towns in Pennsylvania, and like a lot of small towns in the Midwest, the jobs have been gone now for twenty-five years and nothing's replaced them. Each successive administration has said that somehow these communities are gonna regenerate and they have not. They get bitter. They cling to guns, or religion, or antipathy to people who aren't like them, or anti-immigrant sentiment, or anti-trade sentiment as a way to explain their frustrations." As with Charlton Heston's words, this was a politically charged statement intended to reinforce his supporter base's value system.

In both cases, your brother and your aunt hear about and even debate the meaning of each of these remarks, but neither was that different in purpose from the words a general might deliver to his army during a prolonged battle. They signaled value systems, reinforced community, and helped steel each side to its own position— and were ultimately counterproductive to achieving any kind of resolution.

Hands realm: what is useful?

While disagreements about information and value systems are present in the gun debate, it's really all about strategy. What actions are feasible and would lead to positive results?

If your brother and aunt are listening to the voice of power, they might think that brute force could be used to somehow ram new legislation through Congress that would force the other side to concede defeat. This strategy would deliver the fruit of security, at least temporarily.

If your brother and aunt are listening to the voice of reason, then we get into the peculiarities of interpreting constitutional law and implementing and enforcing new laws that minimize the backlash against the new laws. They might put forth statistics and laws from other countries and compare homicide rates amongst states that have different gun laws to identify possible correlations and causations. This kind of strategy would appeal to the fruit of security as well, and would take a hard line on being honest about the true costs in lives and well-being that are at stake.

The voice of reason, by being slightly out of touch with emotions and belief systems that exist outside of what can be measured scientifically, harbors a few naive hopes that are worth mentioning. Your brother might hope, deep down, that introducing new gun-control legislation that reduces gun violence would lead your aunt to stop fighting for gun rights. And your aunt might hope, deep down, that reducing or removing gun-control legislation, and thereby preserving personal freedoms, would cause your brother to quiet down and stop fighting for more gun control. The hidden assumption on both sides here is that some form of legal action, matched with proper rollout and enforcement, would make the argument go away. But if we step back from the sterile logic of reason, it should be clear that these outcomes are extremely unlikely. It's wishful thinking to hope that winning the argument with reason would somehow erase the core values that power each side's position.

What is the best endgame for the gun-control debate that both sides could agree on? Is there one that doesn't rely on willful blindness about how values and beliefs really work? Do we really expect the other side to simply concede defeat once we have won and to shut up forevermore? Is it possible that both your brother and your aunt have overestimated their own side's effectiveness in this war, and underestimated the other side's capacity to continue to meet every one of the attacks pointed at it?

Disagreement feels futile when the voices of power and reason fail us. We start listening to the voice of avoidance—just give up on the other side ever becoming reasonable. But now we know what to do! Let's ask a better question.

The gun-control potluck

When I was exploring better questions to ask within this debate, I tried several things that didn't end up working. The voice of possibility doesn't have answers, only questions, and when it sends you down a given path there is no guarantee of an answer at the end. In my case, I tried inviting people to an online thirty-day gun-control challenge with very clear expectations about how we'd behave toward one another, etc. I thought it was well designed. The only problem with it was that nobody wanted to join. After I asked a few follow-up questions, it became clear that it felt like a trap to people. In a conversation without much goodwill, people are generally skeptical that a productive disagreement can happen, and given all of the other things competing for people's attention, the small chance that a thoughtful conversation might work didn't outweigh the cost. I tried it in a public setting, online; in a private one-on-one setting; and with a private group. The private one-on-ones worked best in terms of getting people to start talking, but they didn't last very long. The other two never got off the ground.

Sometimes a single question can pivot a conversation on its

axis, shifting it from a head-to-head battle into an open-ended collaboration.

I changed the game from "online debate" to "potluck at my house." I changed the goal from "let's debate ideas" to "let's enjoy each other's company while having a stimulating conversation." I changed the conversational medium from "type into a comment text box" to "discuss over food and drink." And I changed the question from "What do you believe?" to the biggest unanswered question in my own head: "What's the endgame for the gun-control debate?"

When I sent this invite out to a fairly broad audience of friends and acquaintances, people were much more willing to participate.

The power of potluck

About fifteen or so people showed up on a Saturday around 5:00 pm. It was an interesting blend of friends from different contexts—some we'd befriended through our son's school, others from work, a couple of old friends from childhood, and a few people I had never met before or who were only acquaintances through friends of friends. Everyone brought a side dish or a drink for the group, and after a bit of mingling, I gathered everyone together and set some very light context for the "experiment."

The agenda was written on a little easel in the dining room:

- Introduce context
- Share results from the questionnaire while we eat
- Share personal experiences from the survey, and any that others want to offer
- Basic facts about guns
- Structured group discussion
- Feedback and next steps

We grabbed some food and tried to crowd ourselves around a large dining table. There was definitely anticipation in the air, because the mix of strangers and a heated topic gave everything an element of potential danger. But instead of dread, it felt a bit more like excitement.

We went around the table, introduced ourselves, and answered the questions "What is your own personal history with guns? What things in your life have helped inform your current position?"

I told my story, about how my grandfather had a cabinet full of rifles in the living room and we would frequently try to unlock the door. One day, when I was around age six or seven, he took me out to the canyons (we lived in Southern California) and he taught me how to shoot a rifle. I remember pointing the gun at a barrel out in the distance, leaning against his truck, and pulling the trigger. The recoil of the gun hit me and gave me a black eye. I also told the story of being held up at gunpoint when I was a cashier at a Circle K during college. The gunman wanted a carton of cigarettes and a bunch of lottery tickets, which I gladly handed over.

All but three people at the table had fired guns before. One friend, Sterling, had just purchased a rifle and told us about all the steps he took when considering the purchase, the things he had debated with his wife about storage of the gun, and the legal requirements in California that he went through in order to get the gun. It was immediately apparent to all of us just how limited our knowledge of the gun laws in individual states was. Even if we were able to look them up on the internet, the myriad details of firearms training, licensing, and registration requirements triggered a fairly long list of questions in order for us to just understand the operational aspects of gun purchasing, motivated by curiosity more than anything else.

Another person there that night, Nick, shared his story of growing up in the South, in a very conservative family. He became a member of the NRA in early adulthood and was proud of his collection of semiautomatic rifles. He shared intimate details of how his thinking had developed and changed over the years, eventually leading to him letting his membership expire. He was peppered with questions and kept many of us enthralled with tales of how our conceptions of how conservative gun-rights advocates think, behave, and act are mistaken.

The group that night was skewed heavily in the direction of gun-control advocates, and yet we quickly found that there was quite a bit of variety in beliefs within that position. As we ate, passing dishes and bottles across the table, and slowly filled our bellies with sustenance, it felt completely natural to also pass extremely different experiences and stories among us. Just as everyone had brought a different dish to the potluck, we had each also brought a different set of experiences and default beliefs to the table. Some of the dishes were simple and minimal, just as some of our beliefs had been crafted largely by surface-level experiences. For example, our friend Erin spoke of her relationship to guns growing up in Canada (where there are fairly strict gun laws and only 17 percent of the incidents of gun violence per capita that the US has). Others had deep and traumatic experiences of suicide and murder. In Nick's case, there was a marked lack of drama or death, but he helped present a rich and fruitful culture that we could relate to even though it was unfamiliar to us.

There's something tribal and inclusive about eating food together. You rarely share a meal with an enemy, and in cases where we do, it's often in the spirit of reconciliation. The phrase "breaking bread together" is associated with resolving differences and repairing relationships. The connection between food and argument shows up in all kinds of weird places once you begin to look for it.

Think of how many years early humans spent around campfires, eating the day's hunt and strategizing the next. This combination is fused deep in our social DNA. These two Bedouin proverbs speak to it quite directly:

The broth is cooking, and now we have to act as one.

He who shares his bread and salt is not my enemy.

Other examples of food and argument pairing well together:

- The Last Supper among Jesus and his disciples, right before he was taken away to be crucified.
- King Arthur's Round Table, which functioned as the focal point for both great feasts and great military strategy to take place, among equals.
- Thanksgiving dinner, which holds a similar purpose of bringing families and friends together in solidarity despite differences—sometimes it works and sometimes it doesn't, but the purpose and context of the meal is clear.

Food is an essential ingredient in the art of productive disagreement. One unexpected place it popped up in my own experience was when I was an engineer on Amazon's Recommendations team in the early 2000s. At the time, the company was growing quickly, from books to music to video and beyond. When I joined the company, our all-hands meeting could fit in the Moore Theatre in Seattle, with its capacity of 1,800 or so. Every few months, the all-hands meeting had to move to larger and larger venues that could hold more and more people. When a company scales at that rate, it's important that its individual teams are also equipped with tools to stay productive. Jeff Bezos famously proposed the wacky idea of "two-pizza teams," which was the philosophy behind a complete reorganization of the company. The way this story is told is that one day a manager at an off-site complained about how hard it was to stay up-to-date with all the other teams and suggested coming up with a better communication framework. Jeff Bezos's response was "No! Communication is terrible!" and he went on to invent the "two-pizza team." If there are eight slices per pizza, and people eat one to three slices each, it really keeps the teams in the eight-to-ten-person range. This size cap encouraged deep and flowing conversations at the team level, while discouraging it between teams—and despite incredible skepticism from pretty much everyone at the time, it worked. By taking advantage of the small-table dynamics, teams were encouraged to do everything they needed to do without being blocked by other teams. They would also be expected to resolve their own problems as they came up, without slowing everyone else down by having a lot of meetings.

It's no coincidence that this connection between food and argument is at the center of so many of our social dramas and much history. Eating together makes it easier to digest the inevitable disagreements that rise up among family members, coworkers, friends, and even strangers, and forces a natural limit to the conversations and disagreements that spark. Thanksgiving dinner might have a reputation for inviting heated disagreements, but maybe it's because the dinner table is a soothing, neutral setting in which to host difficult conversations that would be ten times worse if approached in other venues.

Possible end games

As the evening progressed at the gun-control potluck, once our meal was done and we were taking a breather before dessert, we tried a further experiment: We read some high-level gun facts that I had collected ahead of time. Some of them confirmed existing beliefs, and others challenged them. A sampling of these facts included:

- There may be 270 million or more guns in the United States.
- 35 percent of households have guns.
- Gun deaths per capita are around 12 per 100,000.
- 38 percent of gun deaths come from violence (half are black men).
- 62 percent of gun deaths come from suicide (mostly white men).
- Less than 1% percent of gun deaths come from mass shootings of more than 3 people.
- 5 percent of gun deaths come from semiautomatic rifles.
- More than 90 percent of gun deaths come from handguns.
- Suicide attempts are 17 times more likely to succeed when a gun is used.

With this information fresh in our heads, along with our own personal experiences and stories that had been shared, I asked what each person thought was the endgame for the gun-control debate. In other words, "How will we know when we have unquestionably fixed the problem of guns?" This question applied to people who believed in gun control as well as those who believed in gun rights. It had become apparent to us during the course of dinner that both sides were concerned about safety, self-defense, and freedom. The only difference was in our definitions of who most needed protection, and what people were willing to give up in order to gain that safety.

We went around the table, and a few suggestions were proposed. One person suggested that the evidence of success would be reducing the number of automatic and semiautomatic guns people owned to zero. Another person suggested that we reduce the number of mass shootings to zero. Another person suggested that we reduce the number of gun homicides to zero. There was broad agreement around this one, as it felt like we were getting closer to the true root of the problem. Nick, who had continued to be our sounding board for gun-rights advocates, offered a twist that would feel better to him: "Why don't we just reduce the total number of homicides and suicides across the board as much as possible, regardless of how they happened? That way, you can avoid the argument that a bad person will kill people some other way if they don't have guns. And you can also rest assured that reducing gun deaths might still be the best strategy for lowering that number. But if someone comes up with a better way to save more lives, that should also be a good use of time and energy."

Reading this on a page, you may or may not have had an immediate reaction to this suggestion. Perhaps an internal conflict has been sparked based on your agreement or disagreement with the suggestion. In fact, it's probably not the first time you've heard this suggestion, nor the first time that you've brushed it aside. However, because this idea came up within the context of a conversation that had moved among hyper-personal and silly and curious and technical modes, this suggestion actually landed pretty profoundly with the group. Enough goodwill had been built up to create the mental space for this suggestion to be entertained as a possibility worth considering—and perhaps our digestive systems had kicked in as well, sedating us a bit.

"Maybe," I thought, "it is okay for us to loosen our grip on the gun-control agenda just enough to consider the problem of all violence and suicide. Why not? We're all friends here." And of course, the voice of reason in the back of my mind still whispered, "Gun control is probably the best strategy for this anyway, so I don't really have to consider other options."

The endgame was defined like this: "Reduce the total amount of homicides and suicides by as much as possible, with the least encroachment on personal liberty." It could have been something else as well—suddenly there were all kinds of endgames on the table—but this was the one we all agreed to.

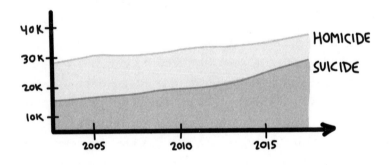

I instructed people to break up into groups of three or four, refill their drinks, and come up with their best state or federal legislative proposals in the form of a new bill. For the sake of this exercise, we would imagine that the bill would automatically pass (you don't need to make compromises to get Congress on board), but groups needed to consider how it would be rolled out and enforced once made into law. I also suggested that we consider results in a time frame of twenty years, to encourage big bets whose effects would ripple out over time rather than urgent solutions.

And I added one more twist.

The monkey's paw

In addition to coming up with a legislative proposal to reduce homicides and suicides as much as possible in twenty years, I asked each group to write their proposal in a way that could be granted by the monkey's paw, which would then attempt to exploit every possible loophole that could make the proposal backfire. When the groups came back and shared their proposals, the other groups would play the role of the monkey's paw and think of how to make the proposal backfire in the worst possible ways. Therefore, groups were to choose their words carefully and expect criticism.

We split into groups for about thirty minutes and had vigorous and energetic conversations—due partially to the fact that by that time we had had a few drinks, but I'm pretty sure part of it was also because there was a time limit, and there was a slight element of competition in play. It couldn't be that difficult, we thought, to come up with a solid proposal after this much context building and conversation, right?

And yet it was really tough!

My group ran into a few barriers. For one, homicides and suicides are two very different problems, with very different potential solutions. Suicides account for 65 percent of gun deaths, so it didn't make sense to just address the homicide problem and neglect the suicide one unless we were okay with a maximum effectiveness of a 35 percent reduction in our main number. Also, the 35 percent of homicides were half due to violence involving African American men, which is hardly covered in the news. The top concerns of people coming in were about assault rifles and mass shootings, both of which made up only a tiny portion of the problem; it became clear that going after those and fixing them completely would barely dent our numbers. What did we know about how to prevent suicide, especially among white men in suburban areas? What did we know about reducing violence among black men in cities? It took only a few minutes to realize that we didn't know much.

The striking thing about all of this was that I hadn't realized how little I knew about the full picture of homicide and suicide patterns in America until that very moment. Others, like Nick, who had also realized this, gently encouraged us to keep pursuing this train of thought. As our small group explored this realization, it became pretty easy to learn more about these things (everything is a single Google search away these days). We looked up ballpark figures regarding who is committing suicide and checked out how our nation's rates compare to other nations' rates and who exactly is killing whom with guns. It seems a bit silly to say this in retrospect, but how naive were we to think that we had the answers to these systemic problems without anything but a skin-deep understanding of what was going on?

Suddenly, it became very easy to ditch simplistic solutions like banning assault rifles and adding a waiting period to gun purchases. For one, many states already had those laws implemented. And for another, they didn't really solve the problem.

So what would? We had ten minutes to figure it out.

Suffice it to say we didn't figure it out. There were three breakout groups, and we all came back together to share our proposals. The first team's proposal was to create a new line of smart guns that would fire only if used by the owner—basically, guns with fingerprint and facial recognition. The other two teams, playing the role of the monkey's paw, played out a scenario where these guns were now controlled by Google and Apple and required charging. Because they had to be charged, like phones, they became less secure, and children were able to trick the facial recognition software on the guns (which would inevitably become out of date due to lack of software updates) and create a few terrible PR tragedies that relegated smart guns to the fate of Segways and VHS.

The proposal of the second team, of which I was a part, came up with a new DMV-like private organization named the DCG (the Department of Cool Guns, to make it attractive to millennials). It would be partially staffed by the NRA, in order to get political buy-in from both parties, and would test and enforce gun licenses in a manner very similar to how the DMV manages driver's licenses. In addition, the DCG would include you in a federal registry of gun owners that also centralized criminal records and new mental health reports. Other small pieces of the puzzle were to create expensive tariffs on ammunition imports and to subsidize a new "smart bullet" technology that would allow any bullet to have a unique fingerprint that could be traced back to the licensed gun owner who bought the ammo. We'd have to allow time for supply and demand to slowly tip the scales in favor of smart bullets even for black-market guns and ammo. This, of course, wouldn't solve the suicide problem directly. However, for those who were considering suicide and didn't yet have ammo, we could train a new army of mental-health specialists to staff ammo stores across the nation, in the hopes that a quick on-the-spot licensing and mental-health-check speed bump would give the DCG at least one opportunity to catch people and get them help before it was too late. The monkey's paw had an easy time exploiting problems in our army of mental health specialists. Due to budget constraints, they became incredibly corrupt and susceptible to bribes, ultimately creating a shadow org of disillusioned mental-health professionals who extorted people, which ultimately led to the DCG's public and tragic collapse.

The third and final team's proposal was to use gun ranges as the net to catch and enforce a nationwide gun-licensing program. They also proposed the idea of smart ammo (which, to my surprise, wasn't a new idea) but didn't attempt to solve the problem of suicide. The monkey's paw worked on this one by basically wasting a lot of energy and funding on a solution that, while effective, didn't actually impact any large-scale trends in gun homicides or suicides.

The evening wrapped up with a brief "what's next" conversation before people said their good-byes and filed out, one by one, over the next hour or so. I chatted with a few of the last people there, including our good friend Katie, about how weird the evening was. We didn't get any closer to answers regarding gun control, homicide, and mental health by any means. And yet . . . it felt weird to say it, but in realizing we knew less—by allowing our very black-and-white initial positions to fade into a spectrum of gray possibilities, and by working on arguments together from a shared endgame—we felt somehow wiser, and more full.

Takeaways

Why did the potluck unlock the voice of possibility in our group when my previous attempts weren't able to? Though it sounds wacky, I believe it's because the voices of reason and force are repelled by the social ritual of eating together. They stand back and allow other primal instincts like community, good faith, and acceptance to come forward. In the same way that trying a new recipe expands our horizons, trying a new hypothesis or belief on for size can open our minds as well.

The day after our potluck, I sent a thank-you note to the people who attended and got several notes of gratitude in return for the unique evening. In that sense, it was a win. The game of potluck is all about bringing a dish of your own experiences and beliefs and sharing it with others, while taking in what others have brought. And we all enjoyed the fruits of security, growth, connection, and enjoyment from that game.

SIXTH THING TO TRY

Build arguments together

A disagreement potluck is one way to gather people together for a meal and a conversation in a way where everyone contributes and everyone gets to partake. I've hosted a few, and they are always unique and interesting in surprising ways, but they always result in an updated perspective that benefits from the strongest ideas that everyone puts in.

Remember how, in school, we were all taught how to write an essay? You start with an introduction that grabs the reader's attention, sets up the thesis, and summarizes your major supporting points. Then you write a paragraph for each of the supporting points, going into more detail and giving evidence about how they support your thesis. Finally, you conclude by restating your thesis and tying all the major supporting points together into a nice bow. This is how the voice of reason likes to write an essay, and it's embedded deeply in our culture—in how debates happen, how stories are told, etc. The driving principle behind this structure is all about making a big singular point and then putting all of your weight behind it. It's a strategic move in a game of Battleship, not an open-ended question to have a potluck around.

The core idea behind building arguments together accepts the standard persuasive essay as a *piece* of the whole, and then builds supportive and collaborative structures around it to give it context.

- THE PROBLEM

- WHAT'S   WHAT'S   WHAT'S
  TRUE?   MEANINGFUL?   USEFUL?

- EVIDENCE - PERSPECTIVE - PROPOSAL
- EVIDENCE - PERSPECTIVE - PROPOSAL
- EVIDENCE - PERSPECTIVE - PROPOSAL

- NEXT STEPS

- THESIS
- SUPPORTING POINTS
- CONCLUSION

TYPICAL ESSAY   PROBLEM BRIEF

Instead of orienting around a thesis, the voice of possibility orients around a nice big problem, which is basically an open question about a shared endgame state.

An essay might say, "Universal background checks should be enforced in every state and for every kind of gun sale." On the other hand, a problem brief would open with "How might we reduce homicides the most in ten years?" and one of the proposals could be to enforce universal background checks. A typical essay would have only supporting points, but a problem brief would also include the strongest criticisms of its proposals, which means it would need to be written in collaboration with its strongest and best critics. This is crucial, because we don't see the flaws in our own arguments.

A traditional essay makes a single case and puts all its weight behind it. A problem brief collects the best proposals that attempt to answer the open question. That means it might have two or five or a hundred different proposals, each with supporting evidence and proposed actions, each a result of a collaboration between supporters and opponents.

When writing a traditional essay or having a traditional disagreement, you might be incentivized to hide your argument's flaws and to exaggerate its strengths, but when you build arguments together, that isn't necessary or rewarding.

Once the problem's central question and end game are clear, and cases are made, it's possible for a productive disagreement to emerge among the collaborators. They can know they're working from shared understanding about the possibilities, even if they disagree about details of the evidence, perspectives, and proposals. Defending against the monkey's paw helps orient the parties in a shared (if imaginary) battle, allowing them to sharpen arguments on each other without drawing any real blood.

7

Cultivate Neutral Spaces

Possibilities have to exist in our heads
before they can exist around our tables
and in our communities.

Think back to a recent argument. Now put aside the argument itself and think about the environment that the argument happened within. Was there anything about the environment that encouraged or discouraged different fruit of disagreement to emerge?

What was the power dynamic?

What were the expectations for what had to come out of the argument?

Was there any additional hidden context that influenced the argument without making itself explicitly known (like cultural norms, shared history, the medium of communication it was happening in, the constraints of time, etc.)?

We like to think of our arguments as existing outside the context of time and space, as perfectly rational dissertations that clash and resolve based on their objective merits alone. It's a very Western way of seeing the world. We're individuals; facts are facts; there's right and wrong, good and bad, winners and losers. The reasoning goes: since the fundamental laws of nature are the same no matter where you are in the universe, this must also apply to truth. We think truth is always true and facts are always facts, and we think our arguments and beliefs work in the same way. The laws of physics may not change, but everything that is subjected to those laws (including facts and truth) is always in flux.

Eastern thinking embraces the flux. My mom is an immigrant—she came to America from Japan, by herself, in her early twenties. She wanted to learn English, and she ended up meeting and marrying my father and having two kids. Her brothers and family are all still in Japan, and I've visited them a dozen or so times over the years. One of the most striking differences that I've noticed between American and Japanese culture is the different ways we think about negative space and the purpose of everyday objects.

In Japan, sitting on the floor is normal. Walls can also be doors. The floor can turn into a bed. Everything seems designed to seamlessly adapt to different uses, partially because space is so limited, but also because Japanese culture has a different relationship to space.

During college, I visited my aunt and uncle who lived in a small town outside Tokyo. I brought a few friends with me, and when we arrived, it was obvious how much we stood out. We were all pretty tall, even by American standards—between five foot ten and six foot two—and all of my friends had blond or light brown hair. We visited a Buddhist temple near my uncle's house, which required walking up a tiny mountain trail. The temple had a tea house, which was a room with a low ceiling, tatami floors, and a hearth built into the floor. The door to the room was so low that we had to duck to enter. This was by design: the low doorway is a way to remind guests to enter with respect. There were scrolls on the wall, and flowers, and every detail of the room had a purpose and meaning. Though I was familiar with tea ceremonies like the one we were attending, experiencing it through the eyes of my friends made me realize just how powerful subtle aspects of the environment were on the mood of the experience. It would be hard to enter a scene like this, for example, and start arguing about gun control. The ritual of a tea ceremony is extremely precise, including a very specific script for the entire ceremony. Despite the fact that we did not know the steps and probably committed the equivalent of multiple tea-ceremony felonies, it was obvious even to us outsiders how effectively the ritual made use of space as well as multiple layers of context, culture, and environment—all considered equal players in a tea ceremony. For a brief moment I could sense how the walk up the mountain and across the garden and perhaps even our flight across the ocean all functioned merely as outer layers of the tea house, but part of the same ritual ceremony.

By considering the outwardly rippling nested spaces that extended from the tea house, it became obvious that no matter how distant two perspectives were from each other, they could always find a way to be in the same room together.

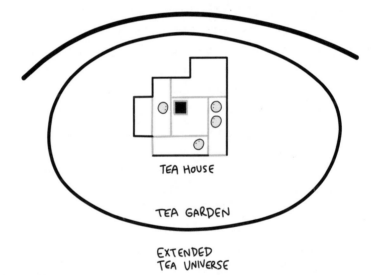

TEA HOUSE

TEA GARDEN

EXTENDED
TEA UNIVERSE

This attention to the interaction between rooms and people is really obvious in tea ceremonies, but it shows up in many different permutations in Japanese culture. When a space is designed to build relationships—for example, around a table with food and drink—it's said to have *wa*. A focused and creative working space, designed to facilitate the flow of ideas, is said to have *ba*. When a space is conducive to interruptions and serendipity, like a park with shared seating areas, it's said to have *ma*. And the context that everything inherits from, including the trips between spaces and the historical context of places, is captured in a space's *tokoro*.

These different "personalities" that different environments acquire can help us understand an often unacknowledged factor in our disagreements. The physical space that disagreements occur *in* influences the voices we listen to (whom can we hear?), the dynamics of the conversation (what roles of authority are people playing?), how people participate (who is allowed to speak?), and even who participates (who is allowed in the room?). When a disagreement sparks in a work context, with your boss, the voice of reason is probably going to speak loudest. There are formalities to disagreement in professional settings. On the other hand, when you're out with your boss after work and getting a drink, some of that formality can fall away, opening the disagreement up to more contributions from the voice of possibility.

There are three things we should consider about the spaces that disagreements enter in to.

1. **Ideas:** Does the space encourage or discourage diverse perspectives from being shared? Which voices are most welcome in this space? Does it have any preference for conflicts of head, heart, or hand?

2. **People:** Is anyone able to enter and exit this space of their own free will, or are there consequences and/or restrictions in place that limit who can enter and exit?

3. **Culture:** How are past and present interactions in this space remembered in the future? Are there any biases that favor or disfavor certain participants or ideas?

Here are a couple of examples of how the answers to these questions might differ in different spaces.

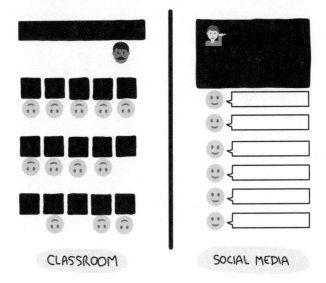

In a classroom, there's a power dynamic between the teacher and the students. The teacher designs the lesson and is in charge of facilitating discussion. Students can ask questions, but they can't change the agenda of the class directly. If a disagreement occurs, the teacher is usually empowered to encourage it or shut it down.

On social media, there are a number of differently shaped spaces to consider. There's a post with comments, which isn't too far removed from a classroom dynamic, except that the cultural norms of a comment thread don't prevent comments from hijacking the agenda of the post. If a disagreement occurs, the original poster may or may not be able to do much to keep it under control.

Think about the etiquette we follow when entering someone else's home. Each house can define its own rules, which requires a

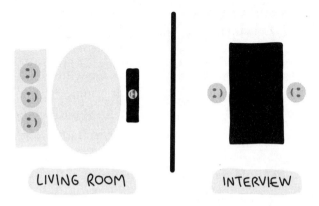

LIVING ROOM   INTERVIEW

dance between hosts and guests to initially determine what is per-missible and not permissible (inviting others over, taking off shoes, regulating noise levels and general level of activity and chaos, etc.).

Companies work similarly but have very different norms around visiting offices, applying for jobs, and becoming an employee. If you're there as an employee, the level of disagreement and self-expression may vary drastically from what's acceptable during an interview or at a board meeting.

Some of the most important questions we can ask, when design-ing a neutral zone for a productive disagreement, are, "Who is al-lowed to be in the room or at the table, and what's your role once you're there? Can you put a disagreement on the table or only re-spond to it? Can you ask open-ended questions, and can you speak for yourself?"

This is especially important when the people at the table are the ones who also get to decide who should be allowed to join the ta-ble in the future. This is what's currently happening in the U.S. Senate and House of Representatives.

IMMIGRATION, INCLUSION,
AND EXILE

One of the most difficult disagreements happening in many countries today is around immigration, which is essentially a disagreement about borders, citizenship, and rights. The reason it's so heated is partially due to the fact that once you're in, you are given a voice in that same conversation. Every nation in the world must have an immigration and citizenship policy, which in turn determines who has a voice in defining that policy in the future.

The largest experiment that I conducted during the research for this book was to create an invite-only online community, fruitful .zone, which was intended to be a friendly and diverse space for dialogue around politics and other heated topics. It's been around a while now, and one of the most interesting early conversations we had was around the topic of immigration and border security.

This is a timeless disagreement, and a perfect example of how the voices of power, reason, and avoidance have failed us. Who can be included in our tribe? Who should be excluded? How should we enforce these rules? And this conversation was happening on three levels simultaneously:

- In the fruitful.zone community
- Among US citizens
- In the US Congress

Each space had policies and systems that regulate who could enter and exit them. I controlled the first level (fruitful.zone) with a code of conduct and an explicit intention to have a diverse and friendly dialogue. US citizens elect people to Congress via the electoral process, and Congress in turn decides on the policy and enforcement that impacts who can become a US citizen, via the federal budget and legal systems.

My code of conduct, the electoral process, the budget process, and the legal system are all themselves in flux and susceptible to all of the biases and problems that result from living in a world with too much information and limited resources. As people immigrate

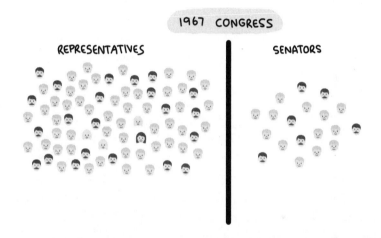

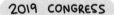

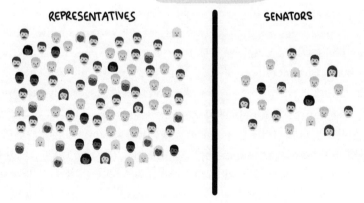

to the United States, emigrate from the United States, are born or die or live somewhere in between, the perspectives available also change, and the cycle continues. Consider, for example, that in 1967, 95 percent of the members of Congress were white men. In 1992, that number had dropped to 81 percent, and by the end of the 2018 midterm elections in the United States, it was 76 percent.

White men account for 38 percent of America's population, so they are still greatly overrepresented in Congress, but the trend is slowly moving in the direction of parity. At the same time, America itself has gone from 88 percent white to 72 percent white between 1960 and 2010.

Consider also that 12.5 percent of Americans are black, and the history of slavery and racism that our country was founded with. Consider also that only 0.8 percent of American citizens today are indigenous people whose ancestors lived here before the country was colonized by Europeans, but there were twenty-five times more indigenous people here before they were wiped out by war and disease. It's no wonder that immigration policy has been a heated topic during almost every era of America's history: we're all implicated, and the conversation about what to do with this reality involves so many people and so many problems and so much time. So far, all attempts at any kind of reconciliation with our past and the present reality have come up far short.

When the demographics of Congress don't represent the demographics of our country, and then you try to have a productive conversation about something as heated as immigration enforcement, it's easy to see how representation *in the room* really matters.

For those of us not in Congress, what can we do? The voice of possibility can still help a conversation happen, but we have to create our own space for it and invite people to it ourselves. As the fruitful.zone community formed over the course of a couple of months, I began to feel that we were ready for this conversation.

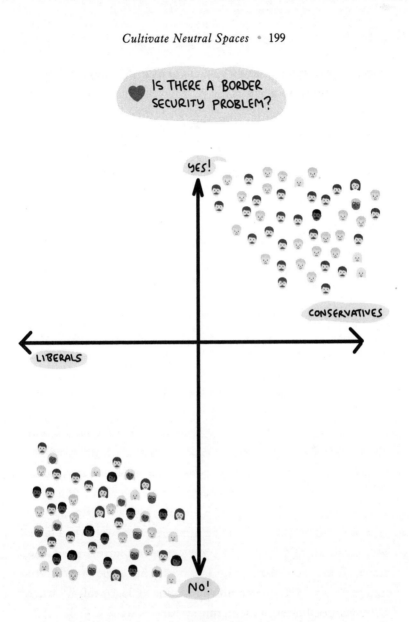

My old friend Jared, a lawyer for Exxon, currently lives in Dubai and self-identifies as libertarian but has deep conservative roots as well. One day he pinged me with a conversation topic he wanted to start in the fruitful.zone community, at a time when the US government was shut down over an inability to resolve Trump's desire to fund a border wall.

> *I'd like to ask a question about the border wall for both sides. The disagreement over funding the wall has shut down the government, and yet it's clearly a cynical play on both sides. $5B is nothing as far as the budget goes, so why is the left willing to shut the government down over it? Do they truly believe in open borders and allowing people to cross the border at will? Do they truly believe that border enforcement is immoral? Or is this to spite Trump and deny him his pet campaign promise, which seems like a cynical motive for shutting down government.*

I replied:

> *I like that. Would you be willing to frame to a bit more neutrally? Maybe we could list the possible reasons why the government is shut down over $5B, and ask to make a best case for each one?*

I learned that Jared believed that making the question a bit provocative would generate more conversation, whereas my approach of framing it neutrally would require people to do more work in responding and therefore lead to lower participation.

Jared isn't the only person who feels this way about the relationship between provocation and disagreement. We've learned to expect a pattern of provocation and reaction in our disagreements, and we think it's necessary to spark anxiety in people to get a reaction out of them. This naturally pushes the dialogue toward where the voices of power, reason, and avoidance want it to be. After some back-and-forth, Jared posted this:

How can we improve our immigration enforcement system?
There's a lot of talk right now about immigration enforcement given

the current government shutdown. For many people, the building of a wall seems to have become both the positive and the negative symbol of immigration enforcement. But obviously a wall is just one potential component of a broader immigration enforcement system. Other elements include border patrol, visa and work permit requirements, employment laws, asylum proceedings, and deportation. Setting aside the symbolic and strategic significance of a wall and what it represents to both parties, what would you like to see changed in our country's immigration enforcement system? Any thoughts on how we could improve the current system?

I was really excited to see the conversation phrased this way instead of as "Do they truly believe in open borders and allowing people to cross the border at will? Do they truly believe that border enforcement is immoral?" In the new phrasing there was no "us" versus "them." Instead, there was an acknowledgment of the complex and interconnected nature of various systems and problems and solutions, and the post ended with an open question about how to improve the system rather than a rhetorical yes-or-no question.

The thread included lots of different ideas, from a number of different perspectives and domains of knowledge. One person contributed:

With the caravans that have come, and with those that are coming now, I believe that if we wait until they reach the border, our response is too late, no matter what it is. Waiting and doing nothing but fortifying our defenses only gives us greater problems. My solution, were I to be asked, would be to meet them on their way. Get to know as many people as we could, so we could really understand their situations. If we could pre-screen as many as possible, we could expedite the process at the border, and show them our goodwill and eagerness to help, cutting down on the possibility of riots and violent encounters at the border.

I know a conversation is moving in a productive direction when I hear open language from multiple people. Phrases like "I believe," "my solution, if I were to be asked" and similar gestures of solidarity are subtle and almost invisible in the flow of a conversation, but they set a tone of possibility and openness for the rest of the group.

There was some discussion about whether the caravans were people escaping violence or looking for jobs, with sharing of videos and interviews. Eventually the consensus was that most of the people in the caravan were seeking asylum in Mexico, and only a fraction made it to the United States, and some were legitimately escaping violence. Jared added:

> *I'm very sensitive to your concerns about addressing a humanitarian crisis. Back before I was transferred overseas I used to represent asylum claimants in asylum court. Some of the people I worked with had suffered horribly and were facing death unless they were granted asylum. But your concerns seem to be broader than having a robust asylum process. If I understand, you'd like to see more humanitarian aid on the front end in order to obviate the need for people having to claim asylum. Is that right? Do you see this as a matter of more US intervention in conflicts/oppression? Or more monetary aid? One concern I struggle with is how to provide such aid in war-torn countries where the people are oppressed and financial aid likely wouldn't reach the people we'd like to help. There's also the question of how much we provide when there is so much need both overseas and domestically.*

"I'm very sensitive," "Your concerns," "If I understand," "Is that right?" "Do you see," "One concern I struggle with," "There's also the question," etc., are all examples of the language of possibility and signal to everyone that this is a neutral venue for ideas to be discussed and not a battle zone. The next question that came up was about the connection between undetected immigration and safety at the border.

> *Has the border become safer? More secure? More able to handle a big influx the next time the Mexican or Central American economy tanks? Opioids no longer a problem? I think the border is more dangerous. Illegal immigration is way down, but the border is insanely dangerous and even more so on the Mexican side.*

This was a conflict of head, so facts could be looked up and shared. Someone shared a statistic from the US Border Patrol:

> *Exposure (including heatstroke, dehydration, and hyperthermia) was the leading cause of death at the border. The group Border Angels estimates that since 1994, about 10,000 people have died in their attempt to cross the increasingly militarized border. According to the US Customs and Border Protection, 7,216 people have died crossing the US–Mexico border between 1998 and 2017. In 2005, more than 500 died across the entire US–Mexico border. The number of yearly border crossing deaths doubled from 1995 to 2005, before declining. The US Border Patrol reported 294 migrant deaths in the fiscal year 2017 (ending September 30, 2017), which was lower than in 2016 (322), and any year during the period 2003–2014.*

The next question was about whether or not border walls work—a conflict of hand. If you ask the voice of power, it's very easy to see that walls do work. Walls are not just physical barriers but expressions and symbols of power. They're intimidating; they get the other side to think twice about whether they want to attack. All of this has the psychological as well as the physical effect of shutting down the conversation. Which is great, except for the fact that we know that while the conversation may be shut down, resentment may begin to build. A wall becomes a challenge: can you scale this? And historically, most walls end up being scaled, and most powers end up falling.

If you ask the voice of reason about whether or not walls work, it might appeal to data and evidence to help tell a story with numbers. This is a conflict of head that benefits from an inquiry into information that's available. Let's look at some numbers regarding immigration and the border and see what story emerges.

How many different kinds of people live in the country currently?

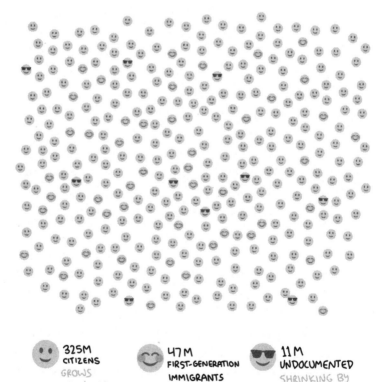

THE UNITED STATES

325M
CITIZENS
GROWS
~2M/YEAR

47M
FIRST-GENERATION
IMMIGRANTS
GROWS 1M/YEAR

11M
UNDOCUMENTED
SHRINKING BY
~100K/YEAR

Of the immigrants who become citizens, 20 percent are family sponsored, 47 percent are immediate relatives of US citizens, 12 percent immigrate due to employment-based preferences, 4 percent are part of the Diversity Immigrant Visa program, and 13 percent are refugees and/or asylum seekers.

How is immigration along the border changing year by year? There are about 800,000 apprehensions along the border per year, and about 250,000 undocumented immigrants are either deported or leave the country voluntarily per year. About 85 percent of the undocumented immigrants who get into the country every year overstay visas from the 52 million tourist- and other visa-enabled visits made to the United States per year, and the percentage of undocumented immigrants has been decreasing since 2007, mostly because fewer undocumented immigrants are coming into the country.

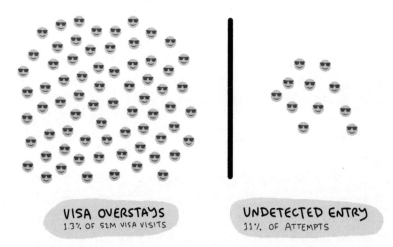

VISA OVERSTAYS
1.3% OF 52M VISA VISITS

UNDETECTED ENTRY
11% OF ATTEMPTS

In the conversation on fruitful.zone, we were also able to find answers to questions about crime, drug trafficking, human trafficking, and the impact of immigration on wages in readily available research. It was a lot easier to collaborate on building an understanding around these questions, regardless of our political stances, when most of our effort was spent on searching for reliable data together.

We found, among other things, evidence that 80 to 90 percent of drugs smuggled into the United States comes through legal ports of entry. We learned that 55 percent of overdoses come from drugs obtained legally through prescriptions. And we learned that the impact on wages due to immigration is small: for every 10,000 immigrants who join a community, wages are impacted between 0.1 percent and 0.3 percent, according to economists. But over 90 percent of the immigrants entering the country enter legally.

All of this complicated our understanding of the interconnected forces at work in immigration policy, border security, drug trafficking, and wages. It had the result of generating more questions than answers for us, and the act of working together to paint a picture around our admittedly limited understanding of this problem became both enjoyable and insightful. It felt very different from any conversation about the border wall that we'd had with people in the past. Getting past "Walls work!" and "Walls don't work!" turned out to uncover a really fascinating problem space for us to explore.

If this same conversation among the same people had happened in a less neutral space—for example, on social media—getting past simple battle-oriented questions to the more interesting ones on the other side might not have been possible, or at least the discussion would have been much more difficult to moderate. Context matters. The spaces in which we have our conversations matter. Power dynamics, expectations of purpose, and access to different perspectives in the room matter. A productive disagreement needs healthy soil to produce fruit of growth, connection, and enjoyment.

The juiciest fruit of disagreement that I got from this conversation stemmed from the reasons behind Mexico's rising murder rates.

From the outside, an obvious factor is that Mexico is a conduit for some of the world's most prominent drug trafficking. Therefore, as a natural result of an industry that is both lucrative and illegal, constant violence between gangs and onto civilians is expected.

Nevertheless, although we found through a variety of reports that the murder rate in Mexico was spiking, this simple answer of cartel warfare turned out to not be the full story. In actuality, stronger government enforcement has led to destabilization of Mexican cartels and gangs, and ironically, increased the murder rate.

Essentially, captured leaders and other high ranking officers leave a bloody power vacuum, causing massive infighting between members jockeying for higher positions. Also attempting to fill this power vacuum are new, local gangs looking to snag a portion of the drug trade's immense profits. Meanwhile, other members abandon their destabilized organizations and turn to other illicit and violent activities that utilize their illegal skillsets, bringing their criminality into previously untouched neighboring states. As a result, murder rates increase across the board.

So in part the murder rate is rising *because of successful efforts to disrupt the drug trade*. Short-term wins can spark new longer-term problems. The conversation participants spent some time discussing whether people thought that the new normal would settle on a less dangerous condition than was present before, or if the cure would end up being worse than the disease—a conflict of heart, more about opinions and perspectives than facts.

This led to a completely new thread about how the opioid crisis in the United States has impacted us personally. It was quite revealing to see just how universal were our stories around drug abuse, mental health issues, and sometimes suicide or accidental death. A week after this thread started, we had not only learned a lot about the nuances of immigration policy and enforcement but had also found a new way to connect around a crisis that has been happening in our country and that was very real to our own families across the political spectrum.

We weren't much closer to solving any of these problems, but we had grown in our understanding of the complex, intertwined nature of these problems and had learned about how different people in the group had been impacted differently by these problems. Like the blind men in the ancient parable, each of us had a different part of the elephant in front of us, and each of us could respect that in the others, making us far more prepared for the next conversation than we would've been otherwise.

It had been a productive disagreement, with a bounty of fruit.

WHAT MAKES A SPACE NEUTRAL?

The fruitful.zone community hit some bumps while forming, as all communities do. I had one situation where a misinterpreted comment about racism led to one member abruptly leaving the community. In the beginning, events like this made a big impact, and the remaining members discussed how we could learn from it. Eventually, the person who left decided to return, and we've been able to hear his perspective as well on what went poorly and how we can avoid it in the future.

Another time, one of the threads devolved into some name-calling. We have a very clear code of conduct that includes rules like "No personal insults" and "Don't post opinions as facts"—the basic stuff you'd expect. But this was the first time we were tested in terms of enforcing those guidelines. In moments like this, the voices of power and reason resort to exile, censorship, and banning as their primary tools of enforcement, but these tools aren't perfect. In fact, they cause problems by polarizing communities against one another.

Tech companies have recently begun their own version of censorship, in the form of "deplatforming" or "no platforming" controversial figures like Glenn Beck (formerly of Fox News); Alex Jones, founder of Infowars; and Milo Yiannopoulos, former Breitbart News editor. The general consensus of research into the effects of deplatforming is that it initially draws a lot of attention to the people and ideas being banned, but then a drop-off happens, after which the banned parties end up getting less attention going forward. Joan Donovan, the platform accountability research lead at Data and Society, was quoted by Jason Koebler of *Vice* on August 10, 2018:

> "We've been running a research project over last year, and when someone relatively famous gets no platformed by Facebook or Twitter or YouTube, there's an initial flashpoint, where some of their audience will move with them . . . but generally the falloff is pretty significant and they don't gain the same amplification power they had prior to the moment they were taken off these bigger platforms."

This assertion rings true—censorship, when implemented by those in power, will be effective. You can look to China and North Korea and even past points in American history to see that censorship does offer immediate short-term gains. In the moment, the problem is resolved. The loophole, however, is that censored information generally comes back even stronger in the long term, because being censored gives information a new appeal. Books that have been banned historically ended up reaching more people than they probably would have, simply for being considered important enough to be banned. Examples of books banned from libraries include J. D. Salinger's *The Catcher in the Rye*, Ralph Ellison's *Invisible Man*, *The Diary of Anne Frank*, and Harper Lee's *To Kill a Mockingbird*. In fact, even as books continue to be banned from schools and libraries, the last week of every September is Banned Books Week, an event held by the American Library Association aimed at celebrating the freedom to read. Banning books turns out to be great marketing for them.

In the same article, Jason Koebler of *Vice* further noted the researchers, who studied the effects of deplatforming efforts against people like Alex Jones and Milo Yiannopoulos, also concede, "It's unclear what the unintended effects of no platforming will be in the near and distant future. . . . [T]here could be other unintended consequences. There has already been pushback on the right about the capacity and ethics of technology companies making these decisions. We've also seen an exodus toward sites like Gab.ai and away from the more mainstream social media networks."

Censorship creates a spectacle and gives troublemaker status to disfavored ideas in a society that values the right to free speech and diversity of thought. We become curious—what could be so bad? If the ideas resonate with us, now we are also aligned against an enemy, on a mission to spread them much further than they ever would have gone before being banned.

We can also watch to see what happens to the ideas that the people represent. Each act of deplatforming creates a minor martyr for the people who were following them. The more they suffer, the more powerful they become as symbols for the cause. Look no further than the impact the death of Socrates had on classical Greek philosophy, the crucifixion of Jesus had on Christianity, or the immolation of Giordano Bruno had on heliocentrism.

This is where the voices of power and reason get tripped up bigtime. They are satisfied with censorship, banning, and exile because these strategies have an immediate effect of removing threats to their belief systems. In the short term, this seems to work in their favor. But if they take the longer view and accept that the second- and third-order effects of these efforts might have the opposite result, does that satisfaction still hold up? To what extent do we remember the ideas of Socrates, Jesus, and even Giordano Bruno *because* they were martyred?

What alternatives are there to exiling people and ideas, especially those who pose very real threats in the moment? It's counterintuitive, but we must leap into the uncertainty this question raises. The wide-open, difficult question to ask is, How we can create communities that accept disagreement, even extreme disagreement, without resorting to tools of censorship, banning, or exile as the final answer? One step forward is to make sure we're thinking in terms of individuals instead of groups as the primary participants in the disagreement, and to recognize those individuals as a collection of positions, perspectives, beliefs, hopes, and dreams instead of a one-issue cardboard cutout. We can't argue with a community, but if we can find a representative of that community, we're able to ask questions that invite surprising answers, speak for ourselves, and build arguments together. All of this is much easier to do when we meet our opponents in a neutral space.

The Gulag Archipelago by Aleksandr Solzhenitsyn is an account of the Soviet prison system, based on extensive research and Solzhenitsyn's own experiences as a prisoner in the gulag. He was exposed to some pretty evil and despairing realities but took a different approach than simply pushing evil away:

> If only it were all so simple! If only there were evil people somewhere insidiously committing evil deeds, and it were necessary only to separate them from the rest of us and destroy them. But the line dividing good and evil cuts through

the heart of every human being. And who is willing to destroy a piece of his own heart?

Gradually it was disclosed to me that the line separating good and evil passes not through states, nor between classes, nor between political parties either—but right through every human heart—and through all human hearts. This line shifts. Inside us, it oscillates with the years. And even within hearts overwhelmed by evil, one small bridgehead of good is retained. And even in the best of all hearts, there remains an unuprooted small corner of evil.

Since then I have come to understand the truth of all the religions of the world: They struggle with the evil inside a human being (inside every human being). It is impossible to expel evil from the world in its entirety, but it is possible to constrict it within each person.

Solzhenitsyn was awarded a Nobel Peace Prize for being an outspoken critic of the Soviet Union, communism, and the gulag system, and unsurprisingly was exiled from the Soviet Union as a result. His message gives us an excellent clue to answering the question about how to radically disagree without resorting to censorship, banning, and exile. It has to do with recognizing that the line we need to draw is not between people. We have seen that doing so is generally ineffective in the long term, and it also requires us to lean heavily on the huge swath of strategic shortcuts (number 7: Favor the familiar; number 8: Experience is reality; number 9: Be overconfident; number 12: Protect existing beliefs) that allow us to demonize others while ignoring our own flaws. We can slowly wiggle our way out of this lazy mental model by understanding our own response to anxiety, developing honest bias that includes acceptance of our own limitations, speaking for ourselves and not speculating about others, asking questions of others whose answers we think will surprise us, building arguments together, and cultivating neutral spaces where radically different perspectives can be included and wild disagreement can have a chance to work itself out.

We can do this by finally accepting that exiling people and ideas doesn't work and isn't in our best interest. It's time to seek out other options, together.

SEVENTH THING TO TRY

Cultivate neutral spaces

A space for productive disagreement needs to be neutral on three levels: it must allow different ideas and perspectives to be entertained, so that new ideas and perspectives can be introduced or deferred; it must permit people to join and leave the conversation freely as ideas and perspectives evolve; and it must leave room for the space's character and culture itself to evolve as it molds itself to the relationships and conversations that have taken place within it. We can walk through each of the three levels to see how they fit together.

DO: Make sure open-ended questions are welcome from anyone.

A neutral space is one that encourages big open-ended questions that take conversations to surprising places. It needs to feel more like a dinner table than a courtroom. Everyone should feel safe and free to speak for themselves and share their perspective with others.

DO: Allow new ideas and perspectives to be truly heard.

A neutral space can be ephemeral, like a post on Facebook or a dinner party or a phone call. Pay attention to the way different ideas, especially unfamiliar ones, are responded to. The space for ideas should feel neutral enough that even ideas that spark anxiety are given some time to be heard.

DO: Make sure new participants are welcome.

A neutral space is one that invites diverse perspectives in, encourages sharing them, and is able to hold a discussion about anxiety when it sparks. That means it needs to welcome new participants and provide some form of on-boarding for them so that they can introduce themselves and have a chance to acclimate. It should feel more like a party than a manufacturing line.

DO: Encourage repeat visits.

The outer neutral space can be a physical setting, like a venue, or it can be a tradition of family dinners or a book club or a series of letters or a recurring event. Physical or not,

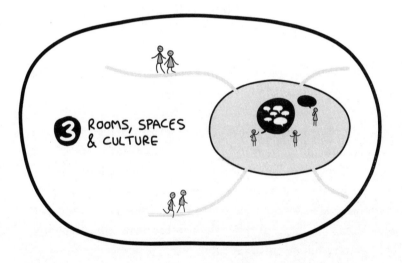

it should feel like a relationship or a shared purpose that can stand the test of time. After all, isn't this exactly what the churches, companies, and institutions that are most meaningful to us really are—an inviting, long-lived, neutral space that allows people to come and go? When you're a member of these spaces, you become a part of them and absorb their rituals, scripts, and norms.

We should pay as much attention to the way we nest spaces within one another as to the contents of the spaces themselves. The quality of the fruit of disagreement that comes from a conversation relies as much on paying attention to who is *not* there, and who *should be invited to join*, as on the content of the disagreement directly.

DO: Let the space gain character and warmth over time.

A neutral space that sticks around can sometimes form a character of its own over time, built up from the shadows of past conversations. Think of it like seasoning a cast-iron skillet with conversations that might have had some heat to them but didn't leave everyone feeling charred. Even one-off conversations will inherit qualities of the spaces they occur in, so pay attention to how any space can increase or decrease your chances of having a productive disagreement.

DO: Allow conversations to evolve at their own pace over days, months, and years.

A neutral space isn't in a hurry to resolve conflicts that pop up, because that incentivizes people to prematurely close down dialogue and even avoid conflict in the first place. Instead, it welcomes disagreement as a signal that there's something important hiding in the negative space of the conversation. It might be information that contradicts the consensus of the group, it might be a feeling of compromised values that someone feels uncomfortable about, or it might be a hunch that the current proposal isn't as strong as another might be if given a chance to be evaluated honestly. The shift that a neutral space allows in a conversation is to give ideas and people the time and attention that they need to grow and develop, which will lead to stronger connections and ultimately more capacity to enjoy one another and the ideas of the group.

DO: Make room for all of the realms (head, heart, and hands) to coexist.

A neutral space starts within your own thoughts, where your deepest beliefs and strongest values are stored, because those are the flint and steel that spark anxiety when they bump into other perspectives. Cultivating a neutral space benefits from some inward attention, whether it be via meditation or private journaling or simply blocking out time on your calendar that's entirely for you—permission to go on a walk or take a nap or read a book or enjoy a snack. It's during these times that you can cultivate a neutral space for the voices of power, reason, and avoidance to speak up and be heard. Each of these automatic voices, powered by our automatic thinking processes, has a reason for being there, and our goal isn't to shut them down any more than it is to shut down conversations with other people.

The paradox of uncertainty

As we have seen in the conversations about ghosts, guns, immigration, and even old glasses of water, when a disagreement occurs in a neutral space, it will naturally produce growth, connection, enjoyment, and even security. Growth and connection are fairly self-explanatory, but we haven't fully explored the enjoyment factor of productive disagreement. There's a certain kind of enjoyment, known to the Greek philosophers as *aporia*, that is a key component of building neutral spaces.

Many of our cognitive biases and strategic shortcuts encourage us to make decisions quickly, because thinking is hard and takes up valuable brain power. In general, this habit has worked well for us evolutionarily, because relying on accepted answers from our communities and culture has the added benefit of minimizing disruptions in those groups.

Socrates is considered by many to be one of the wisest people to have ever lived, but when asked to define wisdom, he had a pretty amusing answer:

> I went to one of those who have the character of being wise . . . [H]aving fallen into conversation with him, this man appeared to be wise in the opinion of most other men, and especially in his own opinion, though in fact he was not so. . . . When I left him, I reasoned thus with myself: I am wiser than this man, for neither of us appears to know anything great and good; but he fancies he knows something, although he knows nothing; whereas I, as I do not know anything, so I do not fancy I do. In this trifling particular, then, I appear to be wiser than he, because I do not fancy I know what I do not know.

The voices of power and reason have trained us to believe that being right and winning are the main sources of enjoyment, especially in the world of disagreements. But the voice of possibility has another form of enjoyment in mind. Aporia is the feeling of realizing that what you thought was a path to truth actually doesn't lead there at all. A shortcut to certainty has revealed itself to be an illusion. The first reaction to aporia might be frustration and even anger, but if you consider that it's providing new information and could be saving you from wasting additional effort maintaining false certainty about an existing belief, it can flip into an aha moment that is even enjoyable.

Socrates taught that the true goal of dialogue was to reach moments of aporia—not to decide or become certain or be proven right but to realize that you don't actually know what you're talking about.

How is this enjoyable? It's enjoyable because holding on to false certainty is painful and difficult, and has consequences down the road. We all know that feeling of being backed into a corner and realizing that we've been defending the wrong position—at that point, the idea of conceding defeat is extremely humbling and potentially even humiliating. However, if you are building arguments collaboratively, discovering that a previously held position is wrong is enjoyable, because you aren't trapped behind it. You don't have to concede defeat, because you learned something new and valuable by increasing your knowledge of what you don't know.

Socrates is warning us about a false kind of wisdom that works like this:

We can easily mistake people who have answers for people who are wise. This is the ethos of "Fake it till you make it." In the case of standing before a chasm that you can't see the other side of, imagining an answer for how to get across might feel wise, but Socrates believes that there's wisdom in not seeing an answer that isn't there and acknowledging the impasse.

Instead of leaping into the chasm, imagined solution in hand, by acknowledging the impasse in front of you, you remain uncertain about how to get across and are therefore able to resist false security. Instead of grabbing whatever certainty you can, even if it's incorrect, you can grab the voice of possibility and begin to look around for other ways across that you might have missed.

This strategy isn't helpful just when we are evaluating how to get across chasms. This loop of looking, orienting, and leaping is what we do every moment of the day.

Look: Someone bumps into you, splashing coffee on you. They mumble something that you miss and keep walking.

Orient: Is your shirt stained now? Did the coffee burn your hand? Did the person just mumble an insult at you? Does their suit imply that they think they're fancy? Do they think you're unimportant just because you're wearing a T-shirt that's seen better days?

Option 1: Yes, yes, yes, yes, and yes.

Option 2: Maybe, maybe, maybe, maybe, and maybe.

Depending on whether you orient around the quick and certain option 1 or the less certain option 2, you could leap into the anxiety that the voices of power and reason use to justify anger and either possible retaliation or simmering resentment, *or* you could step back and consider other explanations that might be more accurate about the intentions of the person who bumped you.

Leaping into righteous anger is certain, and employs strong emotions to propel you to a conclusion.

Leaping back into curiosity about unresolved and probably incorrect assumptions is less certain, but also has no need for strong emotions to propel you to a conclusion. You could ask the person if they realized they had bumped you, or you could wash your shirt to see if it's really stained.

The reputation of uncertainty is that it feels unsatisfying because you don't get the immediate answers that you are looking for, but when aporia is used to sidestep the need for righteous indignation and a false sense of security, it's actually *the more satisfying path* to take, even in the moment.

Cultivating neutral spaces brings aporia by opening an acceptable exit from false beliefs and false confidence. It allows participants in a disagreement to take their leave without humiliation and despair, removing any need for a fight-or-flight response or a backfire effect to save face.

Accept Reality,
Then Participate in It

Things can't be changed from the realm of
wishful thinking and willful blindness.

The Festival of Dangerous Ideas was cofounded by the Ethics Centre and the Sydney Opera House in 2009. It was created to bring leading thinkers and culture creators from around the world to discuss and debate some of the most important issues of our time, while at the same time acknowledging that they are often considered to be dangerous ideas.

The first year featured two talks taking opposite positions on religion. Christopher Hitchens opened the event with a talk titled "Religion Poisons Everything." Immediately afterward, Australian Roman Catholic cardinal George Pell gave a talk titled "Without God We Are Nothing." The fact that these two talks could be given side by side is evidence of a healthy neutral space for ideas that, separately, could be considered offensive and dangerous to different audiences. Having them together, I'd argue, created a realm of possibility and dialogue that is actually healthier than either talk would have created in isolation.

The Festival of Dangerous Ideas has featured discussion on a super-wide range of topics. Here's a sampling of a few from the last ten years:

- "Our Attention Has Been Stolen"
- "Wikileaks Hasn't Gone Far Enough"

- "The Pope Should Be Held Accountable for the Sins of the Catholic Church"
- "We Are All Sexual Perverts"
- "The Rise of Women Has Turned Men into Boys"

If by practicing the strategies we talk about in this book, we gain confidence in our ability to wade into more heated and potentially dangerous conversations over time, the Festival of Dangerous Ideas is a great resource (and warning) of some of the challenges we will encounter.

Giving time to dangerous ideas is itself considered to be an extremely dangerous idea. If it feels too dangerous to you, you're not alone—an incident that occurred in relation to the festival in 2014 illustrates this perfectly.

In 2014, a particularly controversial talk scheduled by Muslim writer and activist Uthman Badar, titled "Honour Killings Are Morally Justified," was canceled after the festival organizers received widespread condemnation for its inclusion on the schedule. In the announcement, they said, "It is clear from the public reaction that the title has given the wrong impression of what Mr. Badar intended to discuss." They were canceling the talk because "The Festival of Dangerous Ideas is intended to be a provocation to thought and discussion, rather than simply a provocation. . . . Neither Mr. Badar, the St James Ethics Centre, nor Sydney Opera House in any way advocates honour killings or condones any form of violence against women."

More than five hundred comments on the Facebook post then proceed to rip the post to shreds.

You have to be kidding me that you even contemplated this racist rubbish . . . As a white Australian Male I am DEEPLY offended by this proposed speaker. Whoever sanctioned this speaker I would like

*to see their employment terminated. HOW INSENSITIVE YOU
ARE . . . DISGRACE AND SHAME ON YOU.*

*He intended to discuss how terrible democracy is and how his back-
ward ideology should be accepted. Who would have thought that
civilised people don't like murder, rape and oppression? Yes, clearly
it's the civilised man that has the "wrong" impression.*

*Hizb ut-Tahrir that Mr Badar is a spokesperson for is known around
the globe as a prescribed terrorist group and is banned in Germany
and in many Middle East countries. But yet you were going to let
him speak? Wow just wow!*

What was the Festival of Dangerous Ideas thinking by inviting
Badar in the first place? Was their intention to condone honor killings? It seems unlikely, but not impossible. When you read the title
of the talk, it's not difficult to see how it could lead to a public
outcry. But was it a misunderstanding or just a plain error of judgment?

I want to make clear up front that I believe honor killings are
truly terrible crimes that target the most marginalized and unpro-
tected members of society (in this case, women and immigrants).
In case you're not familiar with the practice, this is how they're
defined by Human Rights Watch:

Honor killings are acts of vengeance, usually death, committed by family members against female family members, who
are held to have brought dishonor upon the family. A woman
can be targeted by individuals within her family for a variety
of reasons, including: refusing to enter into an arranged marriage, being the victim of a sexual assault, seeking a divorce—
even from an abusive husband—or (allegedly) committing

adultery. The mere perception that a woman has behaved in a way that "dishonors" her family is sufficient to trigger an attack on her life.

These are unimaginably terrible crimes that are certain to spark anxiety in almost anyone. To exacerbate the problem, these murders happen outside the rule of law, victimize women, and are often ignored by local authorities; if any punishment is enforced, it's often minimal. The United Nations reports that about five thousand women are killed in such circumstances every year.

Honor killings are ways for families to "purify" their reputations through ritualized acts of violence, eradicating a woman who was considered a "defilement" to the group. It's the extreme opposite of cultivating a neutral space. Anyone who condones this practice or in any way considers it to be justified would be holding a position very difficult for most people reading in modern society to relate to.

Is there *any* possibility that a productive disagreement related to this topic of honor killings could lead to growth, connection, and enjoyment? The voices of power and reason are very keen to step in and say no, there's no possibility. The fight for justice and security requires disagreements to skip the voice of possibility and go straight to brute force! People are dying; there is no room for anything but swift judgment and correction by whatever means available.

Addressing the problem with force, however, is problematic. These crimes are spread across dozens of countries, each with separate circumstances, legal systems, and cultures. The United Nations has a High Commissioner for Human Rights and a Committee on the Elimination of Discrimination Against Women that requires nations to report every five years on the current status of various problems. It can make recommendations to specific nations, but it can't do much more than that. In other words, it's a complicated and slow solution, which doesn't feel sufficient to the problem.

We don't know what to do with complex and slow narratives because by default we just keep worrying about them indefinitely. This is incredibly draining. One way out of chronic unresolved anxiety is to blame someone or something other than ourselves, get angry at them, and wash our hands of it. Unfortunately, doing that doesn't solve the problem that was causing the feeling—it only absolves us of feeling responsible for it. The voice of power uses anger in this way to escalate demands for control, security, and retribution, and we get angrier and angrier, looking harder and harder for someone we can yell at. *Just. Make. It. Stop!*

That's often our default reaction, at least. Is there a more productive strategy to take?

Let's try to open this conversation back up. I believe there is some evidence that thoughtful discussion of this topic could lead somewhere productive. Honor killings are about punishing noncompliant members of a group, which is itself a conflict-resolution strategy enforced by the voice of power. Follow our rules (about arranged marriage, sexual purity, divorce, etc.) . . . *or else!* Honor killings are a strategy for exiling dangerous ideas that challenge the perceived cultural norm: the dangerous ideas that women should have the freedom to choose whom they marry, whom they divorce, and who has power over them. The case against honor killings, therefore, is not that different from the case against all brute-force methods of stomping out disagreement. It's a case for allowing women to speak for themselves, to be invited into neutral spaces and given opportunities to thrive without fearing for their lives. Disagreeing with honor killings is a conversation worth having.

Who should we have it with? Who can speak for themselves and provide a perspective into this topic that might be able to surprise us with their answers to our questions?

When Badar's talk on the subject was canceled, he was labeled a bigot, a misogynist, and a spokesperson for radical Islam without being given a chance to speak for himself. He was subjected to shaming from many mainstream news channels and publications, as well as on social media. He wasn't murdered, as the victims of honor killings themselves are, but the social dynamics were similar: destroy him for his dangerous ideas. But what were his ideas? Were they actually what was being projected onto him? Badar did eventually conduct an interview with ABC News Radio to represent his perspective and made a clear statement at the very beginning:

> I do not condone, and Islam does not condone, any form of violence or abuse towards women. And I don't condone vigilante justice.

Wait, then why did he give his talk such a provocative title? He tells us:

> The idea of the Festival of Dangerous Ideas is to pull out provocative and controversial ideas. Last year, one of the titles was "Killers Can Be Good." If you want to make assumptions about the talk without looking at anything but the title, we can be outraged by that. But all he meant, when we actually listen to him, was that ax murderers can change and become good people that we should accept in society. Because he was a white guy, a thirty-four-year-old male, American, that probably helped his case. Anyone who read the blurb of my talk would have seen that it was about discussing the perceptions, the assumptions, the presumptions behind honour killings. When the issue is raised in the West, the social imagination goes straight to stonings of women in far-off lands in Asia and Africa. Why? Why is it so narrow? What about abuse and killing of women by domestic violence here at home, if indeed the issue is about violence against women?

His talk, as he described it, was meant to ask a predominantly Western audience an uncomfortable question about why the West is so eager to condemn 5,000 honor killings in countries like Pakistan, Iraq, Turkey, and Afghanistan when, according to the National Coalition Against Domestic Violence, there are 20,000 hotline phone calls about domestic violence made every day in the United States, and one-third of homicides against women are caused by their partners.

In the spirit of recognizing our own bias and being willing to repair it, we can recognize this pattern of demonizing the behavior of others more than we would condemn our own behavior as something we're prone to do. Badar is pointing out an uncomfortable case of it and telling us something that we don't want to hear. We can either deny his claim or find a way to explore it with curiosity to see if there's something we can learn from it. The fact that we give a certain foreign flavor of domestic violence a different name—"honor killings"—reinforces this idea that it's somehow different from the way we commit violence against women; it's more primitive, more barbaric, and more worthy of condemnation. Is the implication that ours isn't as bad? As Badar points out:

> If we're really concerned about violence across the board, humanity in the twenty-first century hasn't seen anyone more violent than Western states. Yet this whole picture is missing, in order to dictate and impose culturally and politically on weaker nations and peoples.

Watch how anxiety sparks as you think about this. Pay attention to how the voices of power and reason react to these claims automatically by turning them back around on him. Isn't this "whataboutism"? Isn't he being too defensive of something that's still a terrible crime, and isn't he in some sense guilty of the same projection back onto Western society as the "other" that we're making onto majority-Muslim states? Trying to walk that reasonable line, the interviewer asks him about whether some things are just too controversial to discuss productively. He responds:

I don't believe there are issues that are too controversial. There are issues that are too controversial from *Muslims*. Or from ethnic minorities X, Y, or Z. If there was a white male making the same argument with the same title, I don't think it would have had the same reaction. The social imagination quickly goes towards what Muslims allegedly do, and because it's a Muslim guy apparently justifying this, then there's an outrage. For me, it's not really the topic. Look at all the other topics at the festival before judging if it's the topic itself or if it's something to do with the speaker.

"Something to do with the speaker" is where it finally clicked for me. A quick rescan of more talk titles from the Festival of Dangerous Ideas reveals that there have indeed been other talks with equally provocative titles:

- "Kill All Normies"
- "Rehearsal for Fascism"
- "Psychopaths Make the World Go Around"
- "Is Torture Necessary?"

Is it possible that some of these talks could be considered controversial and in need of being canceled if the wrong person gave them? Does the topic even matter? If a real murderer, psychopath, terrorist, or war criminal came onstage, even if only to talk about their morning routine, would that be okay? Can we separate people and ideas, and recognize that a person has many ideas, and ideas themselves can be dangerous in different ways than people are?

Is our outrage at Middle Eastern countries for committing crimes we also commit, perhaps even more so, morally justified?

Three questions to help us unpack this difficult topic.

1. What is the difference between accepting a dangerous idea into the room and endorsing it?
2. Should we be willing to hear ideas that we don't endorse? If so, why?
3. Can we invite ideas that we don't endorse into the room in a productive way?

The realms of head, heart, and hands can guide us through this dangerous idea, and in fact all dangerous ideas.

HEAD REALM

What Is True?

What is the difference between accepting a dangerous idea into the room and endorsing it?

Accepting a dangerous idea without endorsing it means that you're willing to listen to a specific version of it to confirm whether or not it matches what you imagine it to be. The idea the public condemned Badar for ended up not being the one he was actually going to talk about. By accepting a dangerous idea without endorsing it, we can still strongly disagree with *our own understanding* of the idea, while also listening to *someone else's understanding of the idea*. Because they might be different things.

The key is to remain open to the possibility that speakers don't actually think what you think they think. That's why we must let them speak for themselves and look for the pieces that surprise us. Those pieces are the new information we otherwise lose out on.

When we allow people to speak for themselves about a dangerous idea, it's still possible to collaborate in making their argument stronger without endorsing it. To make an argument stronger isn't the same thing as making it more threatening. It's often the opposite. If we were previously projecting our own idea onto it, the best case for a dangerous idea might end up being less threatening in the end than our projection. In the extreme case of honor killings, the act of accepting the "dangerous idea" is about creating space at our mental table to hear what Badar actually meant to discuss. It turns out that what he wanted to share wasn't nearly as dangerous as condoning honor killings, but it was still uncomfortable to listen to. His talk had been intended to be a critique of moral justification itself, not a defense of honor killings.

Badar says he intended to "explain the worldview that could lead people to assume that it was morally justified" to kill in the name of honor, and by doing so show that the problem wasn't isolated to Muslims but rather was a much bigger problem that also justified wars, vigilante justice, domestic violence, and more. He believes honor can be twisted to grant immoral acts a false pretense of morality. When we use honor to justify violence, we end up being able to justify many actions as moral that are actually reprehensible. A family wants to protect its honor, so it kills innocent women. On the less serious end of the spectrum, the notion of protecting honor could even be used to justify attacking Badar. It would bring shame to Sydney Opera House to host Badar's talk, and this justifies the outrage we feel and the retaliatory actions taken against him. In both cases, someone in power wants to control someone with less power.

We should investigate systems that masquerade as morally justified but in effect decide who should live and who should die, who should be treated as a human and who should be outcast. That's a dangerous idea worth discussing. I would say that Badar's mistake, and the Festival of Dangerous Ideas's mistake, was underestimating how much a misreading would spark collective anxiety. The voice of power loves a mob, especially when it feels morally justified.

Accepting an idea without endorsing it works best when you seek out the smartest representatives of that idea. Having the smartest representative at the table, in the room, or on the stage is a prerequisite for seeing it from a new perspective, so that listeners can decide if they want to endorse the idea as it is meant to be understood. It's the opposite of nutpicking. Find worthy representatives who have the best chance of finding your blind spots and filling in gaps in your knowledge, and bring them in.

When we find an idea unacceptable *before* seeing it for what it really is, we just fill it in with our worst predefined stereotypes. If we speculate about the reasons behind an idea we think a person has, we assume they're overly simplistic and flawed and reject the idea based on our own speculation. We don't see reality; instead we reject an illusion we've created, which results in zero growth, zero connection, and zero enjoyment. That missed opportunity is the real casualty of unproductive disagreements, even though we feel justified and secure in the moment.

The main takeaway from the head realm is to agree on the factual evidence on the table, the people who are invited to the table, and the shared language and terminology that we use to talk about it.

HEART REALM

What Is Meaningful?

Should we be willing to hear ideas that we don't endorse? If so, why?

Once we agree on the terminology, we can consider it in the context of the heart realm, which is where the real disagreement is perceived to be. Knowing what we know about dangerous ideas and about the trade-offs we make by either accepting or rejecting them right off the bat, what do they mean to us? This question can't be answered with external evidence because it's a matter of personal preference, which includes an internal assessment of your own risk tolerance and desire for adventure.

In college, a few friends of mine discovered a half-finished unused overpass on Lake Washington in Seattle. They loved driving there late at night or early in the morning and jumping off the bridge into the lake. I'm not a fan of heights myself, and tried to get out of these excursions as often as I could. I'd inevitably buckle under peer pressure and go along every once in a while. Then one morning I jumped and hit the water in an awkward position that dislocated my shoulder. My friends saw that I was hurt, dragged me out of the water, and took me to the emergency room. My shoulder is easily dislocated ever since. Long story short: conflicts of heart ("Should I jump off this bridge even though I don't want to?") are personal matters, and it's not everyone's calling to jump off bridges. Entertaining dangerous ideas is much more aligned with my interests, but that's not for everyone either.

When opinions differ on the matters of heart, the best thing to do is to ask questions that could spark answers that surprise us. Have there been formative events in our pasts in which entertaining dangerous ideas has led to good or bad outcomes? What kinds of ideas do we think are the most dangerous? Are there potentially any areas to explore that might actually lead to growth, connection, and enjoyment? How might the monkey's paw twist an honest desire to learn from dangerous ideas into something that is unquestionably regrettable? Is it our duty to suppress dangerous ideas, or do we think that makes them stronger? Who else could we include in the discussion who might provide a useful perspective that we haven't considered?

HANDS REALM

What Is Useful?

How might we accept ideas that we don't endorse in a productive way?

If we've managed to stick together during the conflicts of head and heart, and we're speaking the same language and interested in heeding the call to adventure implicit in this question, what can we do to actually make progress here? How do we pull off something like a festival of dangerous ideas in our own personal and daily lives? What would that even mean?

I believe that unproductive disagreement is currently the greatest existential threat to our civilization and future prosperity. If we can't even get to the point of talking productively *about* our problems, it's only a matter of time until they bring us down. It's similar to the way we think about dying of old age. Most of the time, when we say that a person has died of old age, it's not from some new disease that preys solely on old people but the inability of an aged body to properly face and recover from everyday problems. If our culture has chronic unproductive disagreement syndrome, we won't die from some brand-new threat that is way more dangerous than everything else we've ever encountered—we'll die from some unlucky confluence of regular problems that slowly chipped away at the foundations of civilization until the whole system collapses and we're unable to get back up.

It's not too late. We can begin to address this problem by committing to having more productive disagreements above fighting for any one thing. We can each commit to leading by example rather than passing the buck to an imagined adversary. This will mean opening the table to even the most dangerous ideas and inviting to the table even the people we disagree with most, because it's only by facing one another that we can work through our differences.

EIGHTH THING TO TRY

Accept reality, then participate in it

This is the scariest step, because it means actually stepping into the flow of what is happening and allowing ourselves to participate in a world that isn't perfect or fair, as agents ourselves of imperfection and unfairness—and yet also as people with a desire to participate in a way that helps move the dance somewhere with new possibilities. There's no more reason to dillydally. Take this cheat sheet with you to help remind yourself of what we've explored, and practice, practice, practice the art of productive disagreement.

GUIDELINES FOR PRODUCTIVE DISAGREEMENTS

Join the disagreement appreciation society. Appreciate disagreements as opportunities for growth, connection, and enjoyment instead of as problems that need to be squashed or avoided.

1. **Watch how anxiety sparks.** These sparks are signposts to our own internal map of dangerous ideas. Notice the difference between big sparks and small sparks. These point to our shadow, the parts of ourselves we try to hide from. If left unaddressed, this harsh judgment will be projected uncharitably onto others. Work with it.

2. **Talk to your internal voices.** Most of us have internal voices that map to the voices of power, reason, and avoidance. Get to know yours so you can recognize their suggestions as merely suggestions, not orders. Most of us also have a quiet internal voice that maps to the voice of possibility. Listen for it. It's the voice that will help you most when you feel you're at a dead end. It is always looking for what we've missed.

3. **Develop honest bias.** There is no cure for bias, but we can develop an honest relationship to our own bias with self-reflection, frequent requests for thoughtful feedback, and a willingness to address feedback directly, however it comes.

4. **Speak for yourself.** Don't speculate about others, especially groups that you don't belong to. Instead, seek out a re-

spectable member of any group you might otherwise speculate about and invite them to your table to speak for themselves. Listen generously.

5. Ask questions that invite surprising answers. Think of big wide-open questions that create space for divergent perspectives to be heard. Measure the quality of your questions by the honesty and eloquence that they draw out from the person answering them.

6. Build arguments together. Structure arguments into evidence of the problems and opportunities (to support conflicts of head), diverse perspectives within the argument (to support conflicts of heart), and proposals to address the problems and opportunities (to support conflicts of hand). Use the monkey's paw and disagreement among participants to identify and discuss blind spots in each area, then make them better.

7. Cultivate neutral spaces. A neutral space is inviting; it opens up big questions and allows arguments to strengthen and the fruit of disagreement to grow. It creates wiggle room for perspectives to shift and expand without punishment or shame. It reminds us that it's okay to be uncertain indefinitely, and it's okay to act while uncertain.

8. Accept reality, then participate in it. We can't change reality from the realm of wishful thinking and willful blindness. We can't hide from dangerous ideas. We're right in the mess with all of it, getting our heads, hearts, and hands dirty. The only way out is through.

The goal of all of this is not to come out of disagreements unscathed, but to actually get into them—to become scathed.

Afterword

I wrote this book in part to discover what the art of productive disagreement meant to me. During the course of my researching and writing, an interesting thing happened: suddenly, disagreements came out of the woodwork! When I stopped avoiding disagreements, because they had lost their spark of anxiety, my conversational world expanded to a new set of questions I hadn't even begun to ask in my personal, professional, and private life. I quit my job, took another job, and then left that one six months later to embark on a creative career change. I started going to therapy to make my marriage stronger and to open (or reopen) questions about how we can connect more deeply. I organized disagreement potlucks and conducted other experiments that led to gaining (and losing) a couple of friends. There were times when I questioned whether I had gone too far in my pursuit of disagreement. This art is a work in progress and sometimes my capacity to facilitate productive disagreements lagged behind my appetite to explore them, and sometimes I did go too far and had to do some relationship repair with people. I call productive disagreement an art and not a science for a reason—it's messy! My takeaway is that working on the art of productive disagreement does introduce some potential for volatility in our lives, and that's okay too. If we've been listening to the voice of avoidance for a while, there are bound to be certain circumstances that, once opened up, turn out to be dysfunctional and in need of attention. Of course, it's impossible to say what might have naturally happened in the alternate reality where I didn't dive into this topic, and I'm now aware enough of the desire to protect my existing beliefs to say that the "It was all worth it!" position isn't entirely trustworthy (even though I do feel that way).

The biggest change I've noticed in myself, and which I hope readers of this book will experience as well, is the gentle lifting of the burden to fight every battle—not because you are dissociating from the world's problems or avoiding them, but because of the slow dawning of the idea that there's more to disagreement than who is right, and that in many cases the places we speak from are more complicated than a simple policy position or belief statement reveals. Accepting reality over certainty often feels like a more anxious position to take, but I've actually found the reverse. When we allow complexities and uncertainties into our narrative, that feeling of being absolutely certain that we're right, and baffled about how the other side could be so wrong, goes away. Instead of leaping into battle, we have to assume that others are as complicated as we are, and then we can start from a position of curiosity ("Why did you choose not to vaccinate your kids?") instead of a position of self-righteousness ("You terrible person!").

We need look no further than the realms of the head, heart, and hands, which map to what is true, what is meaningful, and what is useful. The voices of power and reason must collapse every disagreement into a conflict about what is true in order to achieve the goal of being factually right. That's the only realm where truth is the proof of a winner. A conflict about what is meaningful can be turned into a conflict of what is true by treating values and morals as purely data-driven calculations. You may have your own opinion about where the best burger is, but if someone else can prove you wrong by showing you restaurant reviews, or by running a survey of close friends, then what you believe is prioritized lower than what can be proven. Conflicts about what is meaningful have been forced into narrow conflicts over what is true for a long time, because the voices of power and reason have found them easier to manage. "You can't manage what you can't measure" is a common saying in the tech world, and has been used countless times to turn a question about preferences and values into a question about data and evidence. This practice dehumanizes us a little bit each time. Conflicts about what is useful can also be collapsed into conflicts about what is true by running an experiment. It's so tempting to make decisions by delegating them to a supposedly impartial algorithm, until we realize that the algorithms are almost as biased as we are. They don't actually determine the truth as it relates to what is meaningful or what is useful any more than we do. But delegating to experimentation is convenient. And it creates pressure to only propose plans that can be easily tested. It's a common enough error among start-ups that the allure of a purely metrics-driven company is starting to grow sour. These companies produce products that are biased toward immediate gratification and are starved of true character and spirit (because these can't be measured).

The voice of possibility gives equal weight to the head, the heart, and the hands, and because it does this without the pressure of being right, the fruits of security, growth, connection, and enjoyment have a chance to take root. This feels unnatural at first, but if we experience the enjoyment of aporia enough, it begins to wiggle us out of that burden to be right and gives us a chance to instead embrace the possibility (and excitement!) of being wrong. To me, it has been such a relief to have more space to remain undecided and curious about the possibilities rather than immediately latching onto the first safe answer and aggressively defending it.

SUPERPOWERS

When I was able to learn to accept reality and participate in it, I was surprised to find it to be such a low-anxiety, yet action-packed, position from which to look at the world. Here's what I noticed:

1. Disagreements are no longer frustrating balls of anxiety. The anxiety of denying what we don't want to know goes away and is replaced by grief for and then acceptance of the passing of our wishful thinking.

2. I see how few disagreements there are and can keep an eye out for them instead of being surprised by them. This works out well, because I can participate in only a handful of disagreements at a time. I can choose them proactively rather than reactively and can resist the temptation to participate in every disagreement at once.

3. The world becomes bigger because I can enter difficult conversations that used to intimidate me or feel futile. At the same time, by participating directly in the disagreements with my own hands, head, and heart, I see the ones I can have a direct impact on—they're the ones with people closest to me and the people I want to become closer to.

HEAD REALM

What Is True?

Is a productive disagreement still a disagreement?

If you remember the definition I gave at the beginning of this book, a disagreement is "an unacceptable difference between two perspectives." What happens if, after following everything we talked about, differences between two perspectives are no longer unacceptable, but expected or even exciting? You could say that the exchange, while having the potential to become a disagreement, becomes something else instead. A thing we barely have words for. A dialogue, maybe? A conversation? The mere exchange of perspectives that results in a reconciled or otherwise improved perspective? At the end of the day, it doesn't matter what we call them, and different people will have different preferences. Call it whatever you want. I personally prefer the label "productive disagreement" because it captures the potential spark of anxiety that still resides within.

HANDS REALM

What Is Useful?

What happens when we're no longer afraid of disagreements but see them as necessary bundles of potential growth, connection, and enjoyment that we can work through one at a time?

In hindsight, I'm surprised it wasn't obvious. If we're no longer afraid of disagreements, then suddenly the world becomes a treasure trove of possibility. Disagreements are in plain sight, once you stop trying to avoid them. You might wonder at first if it's your duty to work through all of these disagreements—but that phase won't last long if you truly don't see them as problems. Disagreements become part of the environment, like millions of thorny blackberries on an overproducing bush. You don't have to eat them all. But enjoying a few that are particularly ripe and ready for more participation makes a lot of sense.

HEART REALM

What Is Meaningful?

If disagreements aren't scary in themselves, what is?

Okay, yeah—plenty of things are scary in the world! The world doesn't yet meet our expectations on many levels, and in some cases shows little sign of improvement. Unproductive disagreements may no longer be as scary as they once were, but the fact that so many are stuck in an unproductive loop means that until something changes, anxiety and resentment in others is still increasing every day. Political polarization is not a disagreement in itself but rather is the cultural debt and exhaust created by unproductive disagreements running on overdrive. Systemic problems like racism, sexism, the opioid epidemic, gun violence, climate change, abuses of power, etc. are all problems not because of specific disagreements but because those disagreements are stuck in unproductive states or exiled from the table for discussion. Our opportunity is to help them move from their stuck states to unstuck states, so that we can discuss the more interesting questions that lie beyond.

Imagine a world where we are no longer stuck arguing about whether or not climate change is real but instead we are working primarily to build proposals together that ensure Earth's climate will be able to sustain us for the foreseeable future.

Imagine a world where we are no longer stuck arguing about whether or not refugees and immigrants should be allowed into our country or other countries, and instead we are working to extend a higher quality of life to everyone as quickly and effectively as we could.

Imagine a world where we are no longer stuck arguing about who deserves health care, education, a living wage, a second chance, etc., and instead we are evaluating proposals that ensure that as many people as possible had a support system and opportunities to support their own families, and it didn't come at the cost of taking support and livelihood away from others.

For that matter, imagine a world where we are no longer fighting to appear worthy of basic human rights, respect, and support when we need it, and instead we could have the difficult conversations we need to have in order to figure out how we can best spend our time and contribute back to the whole of society and the world with the limited time we have.

When I began writing this book, a lot of these ideas seemed like far-fetched, unrealistic dreams, but I see things differently now. I think we stop asking these questions only because the voices of power, reason, and avoidance have run out of ways to ask them. We've grown to expect the obstacles between us and productive disagreement to never go away, and we use that expectation to justify not looking at them as they really are. How might the voice of possibility help us begin to see these obstacles as the very thing we need to bring our attention to next?

It looks like we have many open possibilities to consider. Following them to wherever they might lead is our next call to adventure.

A Note of Thanks

Thank you for picking up this book!

I put my heart and soul into the ideas within these pages, and I hope it speaks to you regardless of your political, religious, or other affiliations. I don't care if you're a morning person or a night person, a butter-side-up or butter-side-down person, a rich or poor person, a child or elder. If you agree with the ideas in this book, I encourage you to practice them and lead by example. If you disagree with anything in this book, I encourage you to improve on it and do the same. Either way, I want to hear how it landed with you. Let's keep the dialogue open.

Please send me feedback, questions, and corrections via my blog or through Twitter:

http://why-are-we-yelling.com/contact

https://twitter.com/buster

Finally, I want to point you to a reference guide to the *Eight Things to Try* and a *free cognitive bias poster* that are both free to download and use however you like:

http://why-are-we-yelling.com/thankyou

Acknowledgments

I never would have written this book if it weren't for a few pivotal people who encouraged and inspired me along the way. Before everyone else, I thank my wife, Kellianne, for being such a loving and supportive partner. You've come with me every step of the way on the path toward having more productive disagreements—in a very real way you are a cocreator of every page of this book.

Thank you to my editor, Leah Trouwborst, for encouraging me to write this book in the first place, and for being a great mentor and much-needed voice of sanity and good judgment during my times of crippling self-doubt that every creative process requires. Thank you to Lindsay Edgecombe, my agent, for guiding me through every version of this book, including the earliest version that resembled a mash-up of a space fable and a daytime talk show.

Thank you to the team at Portfolio and Penguin Random House for bringing your expertise and warmth to this book, and for helping to sharpen the ideas and spread them farther than I ever could on my own.

A huge thank-you to all of my Patreon supporters who encouraged me and provided feedback to me during the full three-year journey from spark to completion. Having a small inner circle of trusted friends interested in following along made all the difference. In rough order of pledge duration, starting with the longest: Sharon McKellar, Sherah Beck, Ezekiel Smithburg, Andrew Broman, Thomas Bailey, Claudia Doppioslash, Nir Eyal, Sydney Markle, Thomas Cardarella, Tony Stubblebine, Joel Longtine, Adam Tait, Cy Klassen, Kevin McGillivray, Kristijan Ivancic, Adrian Lansdown, Feifan Zhou, Martin McClellan, Chris Luquetta-Fish, Patrik Winkler, Brendan Schlagel, Chad Ostrowski, Steven Herbst, Erik Nigel, Alex Salinsky, Joel Rice, Chris Curtin, Mircea Paşoi, Tom Keeler, Ryan Engelstad, Olivier Bruchez, Manny Fernandez, Alvaro Ortiz, Dario Castañé, David Rigby, Sebastian Brzuzek, Gari Cruze, Ulises Bacilio, Lilith, Ken Schafer, Anna Konstantinova, Guillermo Parra, Natalie Symes, Jeremy Whelchel, Brett Shell, Leonard Lin, Michael Sharon, Wyatt Jenkins, Karen Bachmann, Jess Owens, Shane Fera, Brian Oberkirch, Emery Carl, Jessica Outlaw, Richard MacManus, Zhanna Shamis, Doug Belshaw, Rabia de Lande Long, John Manoogian III, Spencer Handley, Teevee Aguirre, Winnie Lim, Karan P. Singh, Leah Trouwborst, Muneer Ahmad, Josie Mulberry, Oscar Buchanan, Tobias Jespersen, Dean Cooney, Bhaskar Gowda, Marcos Ciarrocchi, Trevor O'Brien, William H. Key, Eva Shon, Atul Acharya, Nguyen Ngoc Binh Phuong, Tyler Palmer, Ioan Mitrea, Matt Wahl, Amy Norris, Charles Chu, Denis Lebel, Joshua Howell, Benjamin Congdon, Nathanaël Khodl, Infinite Jessica, Achim Domma, Wayne Robins, Siobhán Lyons, Lucy Chen, Mary Marx, Maia Bittner, Valerie Lanard, Mack Flavelle, Lynnea Tan, Nathan Crowder, Philip James, Stefano Santori, Michael Ducker, Tal Raviv, Kelly Cosman, Will Fisher, George Brencklev, Christine Donaldson, Adam Waterhouse, Jamie Crabb, Shreeya Goel, Avi Bryant, Jason Shellen, Kathryn Hymes, Fabio Alegre, Josh Santangelo, Linda Peng, Brian Wang, Maura Church, Luke Millar, Mayuko Inoue, Taimur Abdaal, Andy Harbick, Kristy

Benson, Vanessa Van Schyndel, Chris, David Papini, Adam Bossy-Mendoza, Bruno Costa, Johanna Ärlemalm, Mike Prevette, Elisabeth Courington, Donna Barker, George Bonner, Ursula Sage, Jennifer Zwick, Troy Davis, Josh Hemsath, Arjun Banker, Carla Sonheim, Allison Urban, Mark Wilson, Amy Luo, Dave Hunt, Hunter Walk, Kellianne Benson, Janet, Meekal Bajaj, Erik Kennedy, Matthew De George, Graham Freeman, Dean Marano, Jason Bobe, Megan Barnhard, Freia Lobo, Emma Cragg, Brad Barrish, Simon D'Arcy, Tatiana Guerreiro Ramos, William J. Snow, Josh Bowen, Paulo Moritz, Will Miceli, Frank Voehl, Christopher Fry, Ben Donkor, Taylor Hodge, Cheney Meaghan Giordano, Jonathan Geurts, Jeff Few, Sean Hennessey, Anne Petersen, Larry Kubal, Krisztian Dobo, Sara Oberg, Megan Slankard, Jenna Dixon, Joseph Earnshaw, Samuel Salzer, Ali Nurton, Chih-Chun Chen, Jamie McHale, Cindi Johnson, Radu Jitea, daiyi!, Nate Walck, Donna Eiby, C.Y. Lee, Kushaan Shah, Dave Cadoff, Doug Geiger, Yvonne Yirka, Daniel, Ryan Ewing, Razmik Badalyan, Mark Pinero, Achim Mirjam Heger, Ian Badcoe, Ana Ulin, Arick Conley, Stephanie von Bothmer, Derek Dukes, Drew Modrov, Ash Ali, Don Sleeter, April Lott, Yin Lau, abc, Erik Berlin, Greg Taber, Caleb Withers, Bentley Davis, Daniel Brookshier, Daniele Marino, Brennan K. Brown, Richard Howard, Judith Anne Baseden, Saba Munir, Dave McClure, Netway Sa Marc Van Rymenant, whY Be, Ashleigh Brymer, Stephen Bronstein, Jason Gatoff, Cynthia Kivland, Nate Maingard, Jared Riley, Ary Tebeka, Alex Leadbetter, Chad Ketcham, Rachel Sarah, Brandon Wong, CodeBard, jj, Phil Whitehouse, Robin, Greg Pelly, Matthew Xie, Noelle Ochotny, Mark Wegner, Eric Koester, Luke McGrath, Dave Schappell, Chaz Johnson, Manu Bhogadi, Kristy Benson, Sajith Gandhi, Steve Owens, Marek, Cory Grunkemeyer, Charles Cronin, April Oelwein, Scott Crawford, Arun Martin, Roman Frołow, Mira Crisp, Jonny

Miller, Shreyas Doshi, Dipankar Dutta, Kate Kennedy, Joe Heron, David McAlee, and Amit Gupta.

Thank you to all the people who volunteered to participate in the experiments within the pages of this book, or accidentally got caught in the cross fire of experiments.

Last but not least, I'm incredibly grateful for the long chain of authors, researchers, thinkers, and doers that this book is built on top of. A partial list of authors and books that informed and inspired specific chapters is in the Further Reading section.

Further Reading

Not all of these books were referenced directly in these pages, but those that weren't contributed ideas or themes in more subtle ways. Here's a long list organized by how each relates to productive disagreement, if you want to check them out.

Watch How Anxiety Sparks

Atomic Habits, by James Clear

The Coddling of the American Mind, by Greg Lukianoff and Jonathan Haidt

How to Control Your Anxiety Before It Controls You, by Albert Ellis

The Meditations of Marcus Aurelius, translated by George Long

Tao Te Ching, by Lao Tzu (translated by Ursula K. Le Guin)

The Wisdom of Insecurity, by Alan W. Watts

Talk to Your Internal Voices

The Artist's Way, by Julia Cameron

Daring Greatly, by Brené Brown

Free Will, by Sam Harris

The Measure of a Man, by Martin Luther King Jr.

Metaphors We Live By, by George Lakoff and Mark Johnson

Mindset, by Carol S. Dweck

Redirect, by Timothy D. Wilson

The War of Art, by Steven Pressfield

Develop Honest Bias

The Decision Book, by Mikael Krogerus and Roman Tschäppeler

The Elephant in the Brain, by Kevin Simler and Robin Hanson

Eloquent Rage, by Brittney Cooper

The Enigma of Reason, by Hugo Mercier and Dan Sperber

The Honest Truth About Dishonesty, by Dan Ariely

An Illustrated Book of Bad Arguments, by Ali Almossawi

Mistakes Were Made, by Carol Tarris

The Righteous Mind, by Jonathan Haidt

So You Want to Talk About Race, by Ijeoma Oluo

Thinking, Fast and Slow, by Daniel Kahneman

The Undoing Project, by Michael Lewis

Weapons of Math Destruction, by Cathy O'Neil

White Fragility, by Robin DiAngelo

Speak for Yourself

Crucial Conversations, by Kerry Patterson, Joseph Grenny, Ron McMillan, and Al Switzler

Difficult Conversations, by Douglas Stone, Bruce Patton, and Sheila Heen

Fierce Conversations, by Susan Scott

Man's Search for Meaning, by Viktor E. Frankl

Nonviolent Communication, by Marshall B. Rosenberg

Principles, by Ray Dalio

Radical Candor, by Kim Scott

What We Say Matters, by Judith Hanson Lasater and Ike K. Lasater

Ask Questions That Invite Surprising Answers

Anam Cara, by John O'Donohue

Becoming Wise, by Krista Tippett

The Book of Mu, edited by James Ishmael Ford and Melissa Myozen Blacker

The Book of Why, by Judea Pearl and Dana Mackenzie

Creative Courage, by Welby Altidor

Homo Deus, by Yuval Noah Harari

Maps of the Imagination, by Peter Turchi

Start with Why, by Simon Sinek

What If?, by Randall Munroe

Build Arguments Together

Antifragile, by Nassim Nicholas Taleb

The Beginning of Infinity, by David Deutsch

Factfulness, by Hans Rosling with Ola Rosling and Anna Rosling Rönnlund

How to Change Your Mind, by Michael Pollan

Intuition Pumps and Other Tools for Thinking, by Daniel C. Dennett

The Lady of the Barge, by W. W. Jacobs

Liminal Thinking, by Dave Gray

Reality Is Broken, by Jane McGonigal

The 7 Habits of Highly Effective People, by Stephen R. Covey

The Signal and the Noise, by Nate Silver

Thank You for Arguing, by Jay Heinrichs

Thinking in Bets, by Annie Duke

Cultivate Neutral Spaces

The Checklist Manifesto, by Atul Gawande

Creativity Inc., by Ed Catmull with Amy Wallace

Deep Work, by Cal Newport

The Fifth Discipline, by Peter M. Senge

The Five Dysfunctions of a Team, by Patrick Lencioni

Give and Take, by Adam Grant

The Gulag Archipelago, by Aleksandr Solzhenitsyn

Nonzero, by Robert Wright

Setting the Table, by Danny Meyer

Sprint, by Jake Knapp with John Zeratsky and Braden Kowitz

Thinking in Systems, by Donella H. Meadows, edited by Diana Wright

Who Moved My Cheese?, by Spencer Johnson

Accept Reality, Then Participate in It

The Demon-Haunted World, by Carl Sagan

How to Do Nothing, by Jenny Odell

The Obstacle Is the Way, by Ryan Holiday

Notes

INTRODUCTION: Three Misconceptions

3   **"A weed is but an unloved":** Ella Wheeler Wilcox, "A weed is but an unloved flower," *Poems of Progress: And New Thought Pastels* (London: Gay & Hancock, 1911).

6   **nine out of ten people classified:** My very unscientific Twitter poll. Buster Benson (@buster), "3/ The way we argue is ___." Twitter, April 8, 2019, https://twitter.com/buster/status/1115293782491054085.

7   **Today, one in five adults:** Harvard Medical School, *National Comorbidity Survey*, "Table 2: 12-month Prevalence of DSM-IV/ WMH-CIDI Disorders by Sex and Cohort"(Cambridge, MA: Harvard Medical School, 2007), accessed August 21, 2017, https://www.hcp .med.harvard.edu/ncs/ftpdir/NCS-R_12-month_Prevalence _Estimates.pdf.

7   **rate of deaths from the three:** Anne Case and Angus Deaton, "Rising Morbidity and Mortality in Midlife Among White Non-Hispanic Americans in the 21st Century," *Proceedings of the National Academy of Sciences* 112, no. 49 (December 8, 2015): 15078–83, https://doi .org/10.1073/pnas.1518393112.

8   **Gottman recommends:** John Mordechai Gottman, *What Predicts Divorce? The Relationship Between Marital Processes and Marital Outcomes* (London: Psychology Press, 1993).

9   **an article titled "Cognitive bias cheat sheet":** Buster Benson, "Cognitive bias cheat sheet: Because thinking is hard," Medium, September 1, 2016, https://medium.com/better-humans/cognitive -bias-cheat-sheet-55a472476b18.

9   **toward kindness "ruinous empathy":** Kim Scott, *Radical Candor: Be a Kick-Ass Boss Without Losing Your Humanity* (New York: St. Martin's Press, 2017).

14   **Sam-I-Am is insistent:** Dr. Seuss, *Green Eggs and Ham* (New York: Random House, 1960).

14   **Zeus chains Prometheus:** Among the most important ancient works dealing with the Prometheus myth are the Greek playwright Aeschylus's *Prometheus Bound* and the Roman poet Ovid's later *Metamorphoses*.

14   **Darth Vader wants Luke:** James Earl Jones as the voice of Darth Vader in *Star Wars: Episode V—The Empire Strikes Back*, directed by Irvin Kershner (Los Angeles: 20th Century Fox, 1980).

17   **Greek myth of Eris:** The myth of Eris is recounted in the *Cypria*, a lost epic poem of ancient Greek literature (sixth or seventh century BC) that has been attributed to Stasinus, who might have been Homer's son-in-law. Fragments of the *Cypria* have been found and translated by a number of Greek and Roman mythographers, but there is no consensus regarding a single primary source.

28   **Acknowledge the shadow:** John Nerst, "What Is Erisology?" Everything Studies, April 10, 2019, https://everythingstudies.com/what-is-erisology. There's a movement afoot to give the label "Erisology" to the interdisciplinary field that studies disagreement. John Nerst, who coined this term, defined Erisology as "a made up word for a made up academic discipline I think should exist. Built from the name Eris, the Greek goddess of discord, it refers to the study of disagreement."

CHAPTER 1: Watch How Anxiety Sparks

41   **An Old Glass of Water:** Buster Benson, "Me: Seeking More Interesting Arguments," Medium, July 3, 2017, https://medium.com/thinking-is-hard/me-seeking-more-interesting-arguments-8f46cfe845e5.

48   **Ivan Pavlov famously showed:** "Pavlovian Conditioning," in Mark D. Gellman and J. Rick Turner, eds., *Encyclopedia of Behavioral Medicine* (New York: Springer, 2013).

48   **a 1 to 5 anxiety-rating scale:** After writing this chapter's initial draft I learned about the Subjective Units of Distress Scale (SUDS), which is a similar way of rating anxiety, but on a ten-point scale. See Joseph Wolpe, *The Practice of Behavior Therapy* (New York: Pergamon Press, 1969).

51   **What's your first reaction:** Alex Krautmann (@alexkkrautmann), "Today I introduced my coworkers to the St Louis secret of ordering bagels bread sliced. It was a hit!" Twitter, March 25, 2019, https://twitter.com/AlekKrautmann/status/1110341506802552832.

52   **"Officer, I would like":** Dan Primack (@danprimack), "Officer, I

would like to report a crime." Twitter, March 27, 2019, https://twitter .com/danprimack/status/1110912638723215364.

52 **"First of all, how dare":** Zipporah Arielle (@coffeespoonie), "First of all, how dare you," Twitter, March 27, 2019, https://twitter.com/ coffeespoonie/status/1110971520376098816.

52 **"Who told you this was ok":** Kelly Ellis (@justkelly_ok), "Who told you this was ok," Twitter, March 27, 2019, https://twitter.com/ justkelly_ok/status/1110915369286266883.

52 **The psychological term for this:** Leon Festinger, *A Theory of Cognitive Dissonance* (Stanford, CA: Stanford University Press, 1957).

CHAPTER 2: Talk to Your Internal Voices

63 **Eve Pearlman, journalist and CEO:** Eve Pearlman, "The Seven Steps to Dialogue Journalism," Spaceship Media, accessed January 10, 2019, https://spaceshipmedia.org/about.

63 **twenty-five people who had voted:** "Talking Politics: The Alabama-California Conversation," Spaceship Media, accessed January 10, 2019, https://spaceshipmedia.org/projects/talking-politics.

63 **Kahneman calls "System 1":** Daniel Kahneman, *Thinking, Fast and Slow* (New York: Farrar, Straus and Giroux, 2011).

66 **Speak softly:** "Big Stick Policy." Encyclopædia Britannica. December 27, 2017. Accessed June 19, 2019. https://www.britannica.com/event /Big-Stick-policy.

69 **A hawk seizes a singing:** Hesiod, *Works and Days*, line 202, Perseus Digital Library, Tufts University, accessed May 11, 2019, http://www .perseus.tufts.edu/hopper/text?doc=urn percent3Acts percent3AgreekLit percent3Atlg0020.tlg002.perseus-eng1 percent3A202-237.

76 **"Bartleby, the Scrivener" is a lesser-known:** Harold Bloom, *Herman Melville's Billy Budd, Benito Cereno, and Bartleby the Scrivener, Bloom's Notes* (Langford, PA: Chelsea House Publishers, 1995).

76–77 **"Are there issues at work":** Margaret Heffernan, *Willful Blindness: Why We Ignore the Obvious at Our Peril* (New York: Walker, 2012).

77 **85 percent of them:** Margaret Heffernan, "The Dangers of Willful Blindness," filmed March 2013 in Budapest, Hungary, TEDxDanubia video, 14:35, https://www.ted.com/talks/margaret_heffernan_the_ dangers_of_willful_blindness/transcript.

CHAPTER 3: Develop Honest Bias

92 **from a project I started in 2016:** "List of Cognitive Biases," Wikipedia, accessed May 11, 2019, https://en.wikipedia.org/wiki/List _of_cognitive_biases.

101   **"Bias for Action":** "Leadership Principles," Amazon Jobs, accessed May 11, 2019, https://www.amazon.jobs/en/principles.

101   **"High-Velocity Decision Making":** Jeff Bezos, "2016 Letter to Shareholders," the Amazon Blog, April 17, 2017, https://blog .aboutamazon.com/company-news/2016-letter-to-shareholders.

102–3   **"Move fast and break things":** This was Facebook's mantra for its developer ecosystem that was included in its S-1 when it filed to go public, along with this justification: "Moving fast enables us to build more things and learn faster. However, as most companies grow, they slow down too much because they're more afraid of making mistakes than they are of losing opportunities by moving too slowly. We have a saying: 'Move fast and break things.' The idea is that if you never break anything, you're probably not moving fast enough." Mark Zuckerberg, "Letter from Mark Zuckerberg," Form S-1, Registration Statement, United States Securities and Exchange Commission, February 1, 2012, https://www.sec.gov/Archives/edgar/ data/1326801/000119312512034517/d287954ds1.htm#toc287954_10.

104   **"Are Right, A Lot":** "Leadership Principles," Amazon Jobs, accessed May 11, 2019, https://www.amazon.jobs/en/principles.

104   **"If we become adults who":** Robin DiAngelo, *White Fragility: Why It's So Hard for White People to Talk about Racism* (London: Allen Lane, 2019), 108.

105   **Racism is a multilayered system:** DiAngelo, *White Fragility*, 142–143.

111   **"Strong Opinions Weakly Held":** Paul Saffo, "Strong Opinions Weakly Held," Paul Saffo: futurist, July 26, 2008, https://www.saffo .com/02008/07/26/strong-opinions-weakly-held.

111   **"Float like a butterfly":** stockvideo100, "Muhammad Ali: Float Like a Butterfly, Sting Like a Bee," YouTube video, 4:28, January 3, 2014, https://www.youtube.com/watch?v=bNpFiZDqcog.

111   **"It's a messy, lifelong process":** DiAngelo, *White Fragility*, 154.

CHAPTER 4: Speak for Yourself

113   **"I feel" statements instead of:** Michelle Adams, "What Are the Essential Components of an I-Message?" Gordon Training Institute, May 31, 2012, https://www.gordontraining.com/leadership/what-are-the-essential-components-of-an-i-message.

118   **the 2016 election saw:** Mike Donila and Jim Matheny, "Presidential Write-Ins Skyrocket in 2016; Names Serious and Silly," WBIR News, November 10, 2016, https://www.wbir.com/article/news/local/ presidential-write-ins-skyrocket-in-2016-names-serious-and-silly/51-350803984.

126 **"These anti-vaxxer parents"**: Juliette Kayyem, "Anti-Vaxxers Are Dangerous. Make Them Face Isolation, Fines, Arrests," *Washington Post*, April 30, 2019, https://www.washingtonpost.com/opinions/2019/04/30/time-get-much-tougher-anti-vaccine-crowd.

126 **"I doubt that those who promote"**: Bretigne Shaffer, "No, You Don't Have a 'Right' to Demand That Others Are Vaccinated," *The Vaccine Reaction*, April 11, 2019, https://thevaccinereaction.org/2019/04/no-you-dont-have-a-right-to-demand-that-others-are-vaccinated.

CHAPTER 5: Ask Questions That Invite Surprising Answers

133 **Ghosts appear in Homer's *Odyssey***: Homer, *The Odyssey*, trans. Peter Green (Oakland: University of California Press, 2019).

134 **The physician John Ferriar**: John Ferriar, *An Essay Towards a Theory of Apparitions* (London: Cadell and Davies, 1813).

134 **The Committee for Skeptical Inquiry**: Benjamin Radford, "Can Electromagnetic Fields Create Ghosts?" *Skeptical Inquirer* 41, no. 3 (May/June 2017), https://skepticalinquirer.org/2017/05/can_electromagnetic_fields_create_ghosts.

134 **all of their conclusions "speculation and guesswork"**: Benjamin Radford, "The Curious Question of Ghost Taxonomy," *Skeptical Inquirer* 42, no. 3 (May/June 2018), https://skepticalinquirer.org/2018/05/the_curious_question_of_ghost_taxonomy.

134 **"Have I ever heard a skeptic"**: Carl Sagan, *The Demon-Haunted World: Science as a Candle in the Dark* (New York: Ballantine Books, 1997), 297.

135 **The Independent Investigations Group (IIG) claims**: "The IIG $100,000 Challenge," Independent Investigations Group, accessed May 12, 2019, http://iighq.org/index.php/challenge.

159 **Krista Tippett, author of *Becoming Wise***: Krista Tippett, *Becoming Wise: An Inquiry into the Mystery and Art of Living* (New York: Penguin, 2017), 29.

CHAPTER 6: Build Arguments Together

161 **My favorite term for this bad habit**: Kevin Drum, "Nutpicking," *Washington Monthly*, August 11, 2006, https://washingtonmonthly.com/2006/08/11/nutpicking.

162 **In the fantastic short story "The Monkey's Paw"**: W. W. Jacobs, *The Lady of the Barge* (New York: Dodd Mead, 1902).

168 **A 2017 study revealed that members**: Douglas J. Ahler and Gaurav Sood, "The Parties in Our Heads: Misperceptions About Party Composition and Their Consequences," *Journal of Politics* 80, no. 3 (April 27, 2018): 964–81. doi:10.1086/697253.

170 **"There are by various estimates":** Drew DeSilver, "A Minority of Americans Own Guns, but Just How Many Is Unclear," Pew Research Center, June 4, 2013, www.pewresearch.org/fact-tank/2013/06/04/a-minority-of-americans-own-guns-but-just-how-many-is-unclear.

170 **"Today, three-in-ten":** Kim Parker, Juliana Menasce Horowitz, Ruth Igielnik, Baxter Oliphant, and Anna Brown, "America's Complex Relationship with Guns," Pew Research Center, June 22, 2017, https://www.pewsocialtrends.org/2017/06/22/americas-complex-relationship-with-guns/.

170 **000 "In 2015, 36,252 persons died":** Sherry L. Murphy, Jiaquan Xu, Kenneth D. Kochanek, Sally C. Curtin, and Elizabeth Arias, "Deaths: Final Data for 2015," Centers for Disease Control and Prevention, *National Vital Statistics Reports* 66, no. 6, November 27, 2017, https://www.cdc.gov/nchs/data/nvsr/nvsr66/nvsr66_06.pdf.

171 **"As we set out to defeat":** Jared Law, "2007.07.26—2000 NRA Convention—Charlton Heston—From My Cold, Dead Hands!" YouTube video, 1:25, May 12, 2012, https://www.youtube.com/watch?v=ORYVCML8xeE.

172 **"You go into some of these small towns":** potus08blog, "Barack Obama's small-town guns and religion comments," YouTube video, 1:38, April 11, 2008, www.youtube.com/watch?v=DTxXUufI3jA.

178 **where there are fairly strict gun laws:** German Lopez, "America's Unique Gun Violence Problem, Explained in 17 Maps and Charts," *Vox*, November 8, 2018, https://www.vox.com/policy-and-politics/2017/10/2/16399418/us-gun-violence-statistics-maps-charts.

180 **A sampling of these facts included:** Lopez, "America's Unique Gun Violence Problem, Explained in 17 Maps and Charts."

180 **35 percent of households:** Drew Desilver, "A Minority of Americans Own Guns, but Just How Many Is Unclear."

180 **38 percent of gun deaths:** Jiaquan Xu, Sherry L. Murphy, Kenneth D. Kichanek, Brigham Bastian, and Elizabeth Arias, *National Vital Statistics Reports*, Vol. 67. (Hyattsville, MD: National Center of Health Statistics, 2018.)

180 **62 percent of gun deaths come from suicide:** Xu et al., *National Vital Statistics Reports.*

180 **>1% of gun deaths:** Bruce Drake, "Mass Shootings Rivet National Attention, but Are a Small Share of Gun Violence," Pew Research Center, September 17, 2013, https://www.pewresearch.org/fact-tank/2013/09/17/mass-shootings-rivet-national-attention-but-are-a-small-share-of-gun-violence/.

181 **Suicide attempts are 17 times more likely:** "Firearm Suicide in the United States." EverytownResearch.org, August 30, 2018. https://everytownresearch.org/firearm-suicide/.

184 **Suicides account for 65 percent:** Lopez, "America's Unique Gun Violence Problem, Explained in 17 Maps and Charts."

184 **the 35 percent of homicides were half:** Lopez, "America's Unique Gun Violence Problem, Explained in 17 Maps and Charts."

CHAPTER 7: Cultivate Neutral Spaces

192 **the interaction between rooms and people:** Jerrold McGrath, "The Japanese Words for 'Space' Could Change Your View of the World," *Quartz*, January 18, 2018, https://qz.com/1181019/the-japanese-words-for-space-could-change-your-view-of-the-world.

198 **in 1967, 95 percent of the members:** A. W. Geiger, Kristen Bialik, and John Gramlich, "The Changing Face of Congress in 6 Charts," Pew Research Center, February 15, 2019, https://www.pewresearch.org/fact-tank/2019/02/15/the-changing-face-of-congress.

198 **America itself has gone from 88 percent:** Frank Hobbs and Nicole Stoops, U.S. Census Bureau, Census 2000 Special Reports, Series CENSR-4, *Demographic Trends in the 20th Century*, U.S. Government Printing Office, Washington, DC, 2002, https://www.census.gov/prod/2002pubs/censr-4.pdf, 77.

203 **Exposure (including heatstroke:** "We Are Border Angels" Border Angels, accessed February 3rd, 2019, https://www.borderangels.org/about-us/.

205 **Of the immigrants who become citizens:** Jie Zong, Jeanne Batalova, and Micayla Burrows, "Frequently Requested Statistics on Immigrants and Immigration in the United States," Migration Policy Institute, March 14, 2019, https://www.migrationpolicy.org/article/frequently-requested-statistics-immigrants-and-immigration-united-states.

205 **about 800,000 apprehensions along the border:** Zong, Batalova, and Burrows, "Frequently Requested Statistics on Immigrants and Immigration in the United States."

207 **In actuality, stronger government:** R. E., "Why Mexico's Murder Rate Is Soaring," *Economist*, May 9, 2018, https://www.economist.com/the-economist-explains/2018/05/09/why-mexicos-murder-rate-is-soaring.

207 **Also attempting to fill this power vacuum:** Patrick Corcoran, "Why Are More People Being Killed in Mexico in 2019?" InSight Crime, August 8, 2019, https://www.insightcrime.org/news/analysis/why-are-more-mexicans-being-killed-2019.

207 **Meanwhile, other members abandon:** Jude Webber, "After 'El Chapo': Mexico's Never-ending War on Drugs," *Financial Times*, February 20, 2019, http://www.ft.com/content/69346c82-338c-11e9-bb0c-42459962a812.

209 **We've been running a research project:** Jason Koebler, "Deplatforming Works," *Vice*, August 10, 2018, https://www.vice.com/en_us/article/bjbp9d/do-social-media-bans-work.

210 **studying the effects of deplatforming efforts:** Koebler, "Deplatforming Works."

212 *The Gulag Archipelago* **by Aleksandr Solzhenitsyn:** Aleksandr Solzhenitsyn, *The Gulag Archipelago*, trans. Thomas P. Whitney, H. T. Willetts, and Edward E. Ericson, with a foreword by Jordan B. Peterson (London: Vintage Classics, 2018), 615.

218 **I went to one of those who have the character:** Plato, *The Apology, Crito, and Phaedo of Socrates*, trans. Henry Cary, M.A., with introduction by Edward Brooks Jr. (Urbana, Illinois: Project Gutenberg), 19.

CHAPTER 8: Accept Reality, Then Participate in It

223 **a talk titled "Religion Poisons Everything":** Christopher Hitchslap, "Christopher Hitchens at the 'Festival of Dangerous Ideas' (FODI)," filmed October 2009 in Sydney, Australia, YouTube video, 1:43:50, https://www.youtube.com/watch?v=kwiHkM126bk&t=240s.

223 **Pell gave a talk titled "Without God We Are Nothing":** George Pell, "Without God We Are Nothing," OrthodoxNet.com Blog, October 7, 2009, https://www.orthodoxytoday.org/blog/2009/10/without-god-we-are-nothing.

224 **Muslim writer and activist Uthman Badar:** Alexandra Back and Michael Koziol, "Festival of Dangerous Ideas: 'Honour Killings' Talk Cancelled." *Sydney Morning Herald*, June 24, 2014. https://www.smh.com.au/entertainment/festival-of-dangerous-ideas-honour-killings-talk-cancelled-20140624-3arlb.html.

224 **More than five hundred:** Sydney Opera House. "Sydney Opera House statement on cancellation of Uthman Badar's session at Festival of Dangerous Ideas 2014." Festival of Dangerous Ideas, June 24, 2014. https://www.facebook.com/sydneyoperahouse/posts/10152122119800723.

225 **Honor killings are acts of vengeance:** Human Rights Watch, "Item 12—Integration of the Human Rights of Women and the Gender Perspective: Violence Against Women and 'Honor' Crimes," Human Rights Watch Oral Intervention at the 57th Session of the UN Commission on Human Rights, April 5, 2001, https://www.hrw.org/news/2001/04/05/item-12-integration-human-rights-women-and-gender-perspective-violence-against-women.

226 **The United Nations reports that about:** "Impunity for Domestic Violence, 'Honour Killings' Cannot Continue—UN Official," *United Nations News*, March 4, 2010, https://news.un.org/en/story/2010/03/331422.

228 **When Badar's talk on the subject was canceled:** Back and Koziol, "Festival of Dangerous Ideas: 'Honour Killings' Talk Cancelled."

228 **I do not condone, and Islam does not condone:** Hizb ut-Tahrir Australia, "Uthman Badar Interview with Tracey Holmes (ABC News Radio) Re FODI Speech," YouTube video, 6:05, June 25, 2014, https://www.youtube.com/watch?v=buR23MiXZ_Q. All Badar quotes come from this interview unless otherwise noted.

229 **according to the National Coalition Against Domestic Violence:** "Statistics," National Coalition Against Domestic Violence, accessed May 14, 2019, https://ncadv.org/statistics.

229 **one-third of homicides against women are caused:** Emiko Petrosky et al., "Racial and Ethnic Differences in Homicides of Adult Women and the Role of Intimate Partner Violence—United States, 2003–2014," Centers for Disease Control and Prevention, *Morbidity and Mortality Weekly Report* 66, no. 28 (July 21, 2017), https://www.cdc.gov/mmwr/volumes/66/wr/mm6628a1.htm?s_cid=mm6628a1_w#T1_down; "Facts About Domestic Violence and Physical Abuse," National Coalition Against Domestic Violence, 2015, https://www.speakcdn.com/assets/2497/domestic_violence_and_physical_abuse_ncadv.pdf.

232 **Badar says he intended to:** Carolyn Strange, "Are 'Honour' Killings Really Too Dangerous to Be Discussed in Public?," *Guardian*, June 25, 2014, https://www.theguardian.com/commentisfree/2014/jun/25/are-honour-killings-really-too-dangerous-to-be-discussed-in-public.

Index